The Plan Outline

By Jeff Swanson

For more information write: 10026-A Mingo Road, #324 Tulsa, OK 74133-5700.

www.PlanBible.com

ISBN: 978-0-9830844-1-9

Cover Design: Matt Jones of Jones House Creative www.joneshousecreative.com

Archbishop James Ussher's dating system from *The Annals of the World* by Larry Pierce, August 2005. Used with permission from the publisher - Master Books, Green Forest, AR; Copyright © 2003.

Table of Contents

The Plan Outline

This outline can be used as an overview of world history with biblical events as its spine. The date and event references give a visual foundation on which to hang all historical and bible reading that one does.

This outline can be used as a reference when studying ancient and world history for any student or teacher. You can easily find bible stories within their time periods by quickly referencing the dates for reading scriptures that occurred during that time period.

This outline can be used as a hard copy reference to keep your place while reading through or using the prophecy hyperlinks in *The Plan*.

Dating System

An astonishing truth can be found with careful study of Bible chronologies. God has recorded a continuous path of time in scripture. Beginning with Adam and moving through the patriarchs, the age of their births and deaths have been recorded. From these chronologies, as well as from the recorded length of the reigns of the kings of Judah and a 480 year span recorded in 1 Kings 6:1, the dates of ancient world history can be calculated.

There are three systems of dating in *The Plan*. The first system is the AM ("Anno Mundi," years of world creation) dating system. These are dates calculated from Creation forward. Adam's creation starts at year one. The dates are cumulative through the flood. *The Plan Outline* does not contain AM dates. The second is the BC dating system. This calculates all dates before Jesus Christ backward. This also incorporates AD ("Anno Domini," years of our Lord) dates for all dates from Jesus Christ forward. The AM and BC dating systems were calculated by the developer (Biblical dates in bold black, Extra-Biblical dates in bold grey). The third is a comparative dating system from Archbishop Ussher's *The Annuals of the World* published in 1658 marked with *(U)*.

3960 BC - Biblical date

2052 BC – Extra-Biblical date

4004 BC (U) - Ussher Date

How to obtain The Plan

1. *The Plan* utilizes the exciting features only possible in eBooks (Search and Hyperlinks).

2. *The Plan* works on Kindle with FREE eBook readers for: Windows PC, Mac, iPhone, iPad, Android tablets and phones, and some Blackberry phones.

3. Go to www.PlanBible.com and click on "Purchase NIV or KJV." Next download and register free device application (third box down on left of Amazon page) using your Amazon account. Then purchase eBook and it will transfer to your registered device. (eReader support 1-866-321-8851)

I. CREATION - THE BEGINNING: *Before Time - Fall of Humanity*

A. BEFORE TIME - GOD THE LOVING FATHER

    1. GOD IS LOVE

    2. JESUS NAMED BEFORE ALL CREATION

    3. WISDOM BEFORE ALL ELSE

    4. THE PLAN – GOD DWELLING WITH HIS PEOPLE

    5. ORIGIN OF CREATION, ALL THINGS CREATED THROUGH CHRIST JESUS

B. DAY ONE - CREATION OF HEAVEN

    1. GOD'S 7,000 YEAR PLAN BEGINS

    2. TIME BEGINS THE FIRST DAY - HEAVEN (THE ABODE OF GOD THE FATHER)

(FIRST LITERAL 24 HOUR DAY)

Sunday September 15, 3960 BC, *Sunday October 23, 4004 BC (U)*

    3. WISDOM WHEN HEAVEN WAS SET

    4. GOD CREATES LUCIFER (SATAN) IN HEAVEN

    5. ANGELIC HOST (ARMY MADE FOR WAR) CREATED IN HEAVEN

    6. HUMANITY'S SPIRIT CREATED IN HEAVEN

    7. GOD'S THRONE IN HEAVEN

C. DAY ONE CONTINUES - CREATION OF EARTH

(STILL FIRST LITERAL 24 HOUR DAY)

(THE FIRST LAW OF THERMODYNAMICS INITIATED)

Sunday September 15, 3960 BC, *Sunday October 23, 4004 BC (U)*

    1. DARKNESS CREATED (DARK MATTER)

    2. PHYSICAL LIGHT CREATED BY COMMAND OF FAITH - THE PHOTON

    3. THE EARTH'S FOUNDATION CREATED

    4. WATER CREATED

    5. GOD SEPARATES THE LIGHT FROM THE DARKNESS

    6. THE HOLY SPIRIT ABOVE THE WATERS

    7. THE FIRST DAY COMPLETED

D. DAY TWO OF CREATION (HOURS 24-48)

    1. SECOND DAY ON EARTH - THE WATERY VAULT CREATED

(MANTLE COOLED)

Monday September 16, 3960 BC, *Monday October 24, 4004 BC (U)*

    2. SECOND DAY IN HEAVEN

    3. DAY TWO COMPLETE (THE ONLY CREATION DAY NOT CALLED GOOD)

E. DAY THREE OF CREATION (HOURS 48-72)

    1. DRY LAND APPEARED, ONE PLACE AS A SUPERCONTINENT

Tuesday September 17, 3960 BC, *Tuesday October 25, 4004 BC (U)*

    2. PLANTS CREATED

F. DAY FOUR OF CREATION (HOURS 72-96)

    1. THE STARS CREATED

Wednesday September 18, 3960 BC, *Wednesday October 26, 4004 BC (U)*

    2. THE STARS SET IN THE VAULT (EXPANSE) FOR HUMANITY TO SEE

    3. THE SUN AND MOON CREATED

    4. GOD STRETCHES THE HEAVENS OVER A VAST DISTANCE OF THE UNIVERSE

G. DAY FIVE OF CREATION (HOURS 96-120)

    1. FISH, BIRDS, AND TANNIYN (MARINE DINOSAURS) CREATED

Thursday September 19, 3960 BC, *Thursday October 27, 4004 BC (U)*

H. DAY SIX OF CREATION (HOURS 120-144)

    1. ANIMALS, INCLUDING LAND DINOSAURS

Friday September 20, 3960 BC, *Friday October 28, 4004 BC (U)*

    2. ADAM FORMED (63RD GEN TO JESUS, BY JOSEPH'S LINEAGE)

    (76 GENERATIONS TO JESUS, BY MARY'S LINEAGE)

    (CREATED OF FULLY MATURE AGE - ACCORDING TO TRADITION SPOKE HEBREW)

I. HUMANITY'S DOMINION - ADAM HAS LORDSHIP OF THE EARTH
(FIRST DISPENSATION - INNOCENCE)

    1. GOD OWNS EVERYTHING

    2. HUMANITY'S 6,000 YEAR LEASE OVER THE EARTH BEGINS

J. DAY SEVEN OF CREATION (HOURS 144-168)

    1. SABBATH REST

Saturday September 21, 3960 BC, *Saturday October 29, 4004 BC (U)*

K. AFTER THE WEEK OF CREATION

    1. ADAM PLACED IN THE GARDEN OF EDEN

    (FIRST COVENANT - EDENIC)

    2. ANIMALS NAMED

    3. GOD FORMS WOMAN

    4. RIGHTEOUS REWARD OF THE DISPENSATION OF INNOCENCE

II. CORRUPTION - THE FALL: *Fall of Humanity - 2304 BC*

A. THE FALL OF HUMANITY - SATAN GIVEN LORDSHIP
(THE SECOND LAW OF THERMODYNAMICS INITIATED)
   1. HUMANITY'S SINFUL RESPONSE DURING INNOCENCE DISPENSATION

B. CONSEQUENCES OF THE FALL
(SECOND DISPENSATION-CONSCIENCE)
   1. ADAM STILL RULES THE EARTH UNDER SATAN'S LORDSHIP
3960-3595 BC
   2. JUDGMENT FOR SINFUL RESPONSE DURING INNOCENCE DISPENSATION
(SECOND COVENANT - ADAMIC)
   3. THE CEDARS OF LEBANON - SUPPLY OUTSIDE THE GARDEN

C. PREFLOOD CIVILIZATION
   1. THE CONSUMMATION OF ADAM AND EVE
   2. ADAM AND EVE'S CHILDREN
   3. ADAM'S GENEALOGIES - CAIN'S WICKED LINEAGE
   4. ADAM'S GENEALOGIES - SETH'S RIGHTEOUS LINEAGE
3830 BC, *3874 BC (U)*
   5. IDOLATRY BEGINS
   6. ADAM'S GENEALOGIES - KENAN BORN (CAINAN) (60TH GEN TO JESUS)
3635 BC, *3679 BC (U)*
   7. CONSEQUENCES OF IDOLATRY
   8. KENAN RULES THE EARTH BY WISDOM - SECOND RULER (322 YEARS)
3595-3273 BC
   9. ADAM'S GENEALOGIES - MAHALALEL BORN (59TH GEN TO JESUS)
3500 BC, *3544 BC (U)*
   10. FALLEN ANGELS DESCEND TO EARTH AND MARRY DAUGHTERS OF MEN
   11. ADAM'S GENEALOGIES - ENOCH BORN (57TH GEN TO JESUS)
3338 BC, *3382 BC (U)*
   12. ENOCH'S LIFE
3273-2973 BC
   13. ADAM'S GENEALOGIES - LAMECH BORN (55TH GEN TO JESUS)
3086 BC, *3130 BC (U)*
   14. ADAM DIES (930 YEARS)
3030 BC, *3074 BC (U)*
   15. CAIN DIES BY ACCIDENT OF LAMECH (CAIN'S LINEAGE)
   16. ENOCH RAPTURED (365 YEARS)

2973 BC, *3017 BC (U)*

       17. METHUSELAH RULES THE EARTH - FOURTH RULER (669 YEARS)

2973-2304 BC

       18. SETH DIES (912 YEARS)

2918 BC, *2962 BC (U)*

       19. FAMINE CAUSED BY IDOLATRY, MURDER AND THEFT

2906 BC

       20. THE DAYS OF NOAH

2904 BC, *2948 BC (U)*

       21. LAMECH'S OTHER CHILDREN

       22. ENOSH DIES (905 YEARS)

2820 BC, *2864 BC (U)*

       23. KENAN DIES (910 YEARS)

2725 BC, *2769 BC (U)*

       24. MAHALALEL DIES (895 YEARS)

2670 BC, *2714 BC (U)*

       25. JARED DIES (962 YEARS)

2538 BC, *2582 BC (U)*

       26. GIANTS ARE PROMINENT IN THE CORRUPT CIVILIZATION

       (120 YEARS BEFORE THE FLOOD)

2423-2303 BC, *2469-2349 BC (U)*

       27. NOAH'S SONS

2404 BC, *2448 BC (U)*

       28. LAMECH DIES (777 YEARS)

2309 BC, *2353 BC (U)*

       29. INSTRUCTIONS FOR CONSTRUCTION OF THE ARK

2308 BC

       30. METHUSELAH DIES (969 YEARS)

2304 BC, *2349 BC (U)*

A. THE GLOBAL FLOOD

1. THE ARK IS FILLED

2304 BC, *2349 BC (U)*

2. JUDGMENT FOR SINFUL RESPONSE DURING CONSCIENCE DISPENSATION

2303 BC

3. THE CONTINENTS SPREAD APART

2303 BC

4. THE ARK GROUNDED

2303 BC, *2349 BC (U)*

5. LAND SEEN

2303 BC, *2349 BC (U)*

6. RIGHTEOUS REWARD FROM DISPENSATION OF CONSCIENCE

2303 BC

NOAH RULES THE EARTH - FIFTH RULER

B. THE POST FLOOD WORLD - THE ARCHEOLOGICAL RECORD BEGINS

(THIRD DISPENSATION - HUMAN GOVERNMENT)

(THIRD COVENANT - NOAHIC)

1. GOD'S COVENANT WITH NOAH

2303 BC, *2349 BC (U)*

2. REVELATION FOR HUMAN GOVERNMENT DISPENSATION

3. GOD'S CREATION RESHAPED PROVIDES FOR ALL CREATURES

4. NOAH'S GENEALOGIES - ARPHAXAD BORN (52ND GEN TO JESUS)

2302 BC, *2346 BC (U)*

5. CURSE OF CANAAN

6. FIRST CITIES BUILT BY NOAH'S SONS AFTER THE FLOOD

C. THE ICE AGE BEGINS - THE SONS OF NOAH

1. HEAVY PRECIPITATION WHILE NEW EARTH STABILIZES CLIMATE

2. THE TABLE OF NATIONS

(GOD DETERMINES THE TIME AND PLACE OF EACH PERSON)

2267 BC, *2311 BC (U)*

3. THE FERTILE CRESCENT POPULATED

4. PELEG AND JOKTAN BORN TO EBER (49TH GEN TO JESUS)

2203 BC, *2247 BC (U)*

5. PELEG'S LINEAGE

2173 BC, *2217 BC (U)*

IV. CONFUSION - THE TOWER OF BABEL: *2052-1957 BC*

A. ONE LANGUAGE (HEBREW ACCORDING TO TRADITION)

1. NIMROD BORN (GRANDSON OF HAM)

2052 BC

2. TERAH'S SONS NAHOR II AND HARAN BORN (TWINS)

2044 BC, 2056 BC (U)

3. NIMROD THE MIGHTY HUNTER (PUTS ON ADAM'S GARMENTS)

2032 BC

4. NIMROD THE MIGHTY WARRIOR

2022 BC

WORLD SUPREMACY BELONGS TO NIMROD - SIXTH RULER

5. HARAN'S SON LOT BORN

2013 BC

6. ABRAM BORN (44TH GEN TO JESUS)

2012 BC, *1966 BC (U)*

B. TOWER OF BABEL

c. 2002-1968 BC, 2242 BC (U)

1. HUMANITY'S SINFUL RESPONSE DURING HUMAN GOVERNMENT DISPENSATION
2. DAUGHTERS OF HARAN (ABRAM'S BROTHER)

2002 BC

3. ALL PEOPLE WORSHIPED IDOLS EXCEPT NOAH AND HIS HOUSEHOLD
4. JUDGMENT FOR SINFUL RESPONSE DURING HUMAN GOVERNMENT DISPENSATION

c. 1968 BC

5. DISPERSION OF THE NATIONS

c. 1968 BC, 2188 BC (U)

C. NIMROD'S KINGDOM (BABYLON FOUNDED) IN SHINAR (SUMER)

1. NIMROD STARTS BUILDING FOUR CITIES

1964 BC

2. ASSYRIA FOUNDED BY ASHUR, SECOND SON OF SHEM
3. KEDORLAOMER IS KING OF ELAM (PERSIA)

1964 BC, *1925 BC (U)*

4. THE EARTH NOW SEPARATED DEMOGRAPHICALLY

1964 BC, *2008 BC (U)*

5. NAHOR I DIES (148 YEARS)

1963 BC, *2007 BC (U)*

6. HARAN DIES IN FIRE

1962 BC

7. ABRAM MARRIES SARAI

8. NIMROD DREAMS THAT ABRAM'S SEED WILL KILL HIM ONE DAY

1960 BC

9. TERAH AND ABRAM TRAVEL FROM UR TO HARRAN

1960-1957 BC, 1922 BC (U)

10. RIGHTEOUS REWARD FROM DISPENSATION OF HUMAN GOVERNMENT

A. THE PROMISE TO ABRAM

(FOURTH DISPENSATION - PROMISE)

1. THE CALL OF ABRAM TO LEAVE TERAH

*1957 BC, **1922 BC (U)***

2. ABRAM LEAVES HARRAN FOR CANAAN THE FIRST TIME (17 YEARS)

1957-1940 BC

3. NOAH DIES (950 YEARS)

***1954 BC,** 1998 BC (U)*

4. REBELLION OF SODOM AND GOMORRAH

*1952 BC, **1913 BC (U)***

5. NAHOR II'S CHILDREN BORN (FIRST POST TOWER GENERATION)

6. NIMROD (AMRAPHEL) IS DEFEATED BY KEDORLAOMER

1947 BC

WORLD SUPREMACY BELONGS TO KEDORLAOMER

7. HEBRON BUILT

8. THE PROMISE TO ABRAM RENEWED

1942 BC

9. ABRAM LEAVES FOR CANAAN (SECOND TIME) AT AGE 75

***1937 BC,** 1921 BC (U)*

10. ABRAM IN HEBRON

11. ABRAM IN ZOAN EGYPT (TANIS)

***1937 BC,** 1921 BC (U)*

12. ABRAM DECEIVES PHARAOH (SENEFERU) ABOUT HIS WIFE

1920 BC (U)

13. ABRAM'S RAPPORT WITH LOT

14. THE PROMISE REMEMBERED, ABRAM WALKS THE WHOLE PROMISE LAND

15. THE KINGS' WAR

1934 BC

16. ABRAM RESCUES LOT - KEDORLAOMER DEFEATED

17. ABRAM AND THE KING OF SODOM

NEW ORDER OF KING PRIEST BEGINS

18. ABRAM AND THE KING OF SALEM - MELCHIZEDEK (SHEM AT JERUSALEM)

19. GOD'S PROMISE RENEWED WITH ABRAM GIVEN IN DETAIL

20. REU DIES (239 YEARS)

***1934 BC,** 1978 BC (U)*

21. ABRAM'S HUMAN ATTEMPT TO FULFILL THE PROMISE

1927 BC, *1911 BC (U)*

    22. KITTIM (ANCIENT ROME) DEFEATS TUBAL (ANCIENT TUSCANY)

1921 BC

    23. GOD'S COVENANT WITH ABRAM

    (FOURTH COVENANT - ABRAHAMIC)

1913 BC, *1897 BC (U)*

    24. THE THREE VISITORS FROM HEAVEN - JESUS AND TWO ANGELS

    25. JUDGMENT OF SODOM AND GOMORRAH

1897 BC (U)

    26. LOT AND TWO DAUGHTERS ESCAPE TO THE CAVE OF ADULLAM

    27. ABRAHAM AND ABIMELEK

1912 BC, *1897 BC (U)*

    28. MOAB AND AMMON BORN BY LOT AND HIS DAUGHTERS

1896 BC (U)

   B. ISAAC

    1. ISAAC BORN (43RD GEN TO JESUS)

1912 BC, *1896 BC (U)*

    2. SERUG DIES (230 YEARS)

1911 BC, *1955 BC (U)*

    3. ISAAC AND ISHMAEL IN CONFLICT

1907-1507 BC, *1891-1491 BC (U)*

    4. THE TREATY AT BEERSHEBA

    5. REBEKAH BORN (GRANDDAUGHTER OF NAHOR II BY MILKAH)

1885 BC

    6. ISHMAEL'S SONS - DESCENDANTS OF HAGAR

    7. TERAH DIES (205 YEARS)

1877 BC, *1921 BC (U)*

    8. ABRAHAM TESTED TO SACRIFICE ISAAC

1875 BC, *1871 BC (U)*

    9. SARAH DIES BEFORE ABRAHAM RETURNS WITH ISAAC (127 YEARS)

1875 BC, *1859 BC (U)*

    10. LOT DIES (140 YEARS)

1873 BC

    11. NAHOR II DIES (172 YEARS)

1872 BC

    12. ISAAC AND REBEKAH

    13. WEDDING FOR ISAAC AND REBEKAH

1872 BC, *1856 BC (U)*

14. ABRAHAM MARRIES KETURAH

15. ARPHAXAD DIES (438 YEARS)

1864 BC, *1908 BC (U)*

16. TWO GIANT NATIONS DESTROYED

C. JACOB

1. ESAU AND JACOB BORN (42ND GEN TO JESUS)

1852 BC, *1836 BC (U)*

2. THE TWINS GROW UP

3. ISAAC IS ABRAHAM'S SOLE HEIR

4. ABRAHAM DIES (175 YEARS)

1837 BC, *1821 BC (U)*

5. NIMROD (AMRAPHEL) DIES (215 YEARS)

1837 BC

6. ESAU SELLS HIS BIRTHRIGHT

1837 BC

7. NOAH'S DESCENDANTS CONTINUE

8. ISAAC'S LIFE

9. SHELAH DIES (433 YEARS)

1834 BC, *1878 BC (U)*

10. SHAMSHI-ADAD RULES ASSYRIA

11. ESAU'S FIRST WIFE JUDITH THE HITTITE (CANAANITE)

1812 BC, *1796 BC (U)*

12. SHEM DIES (600 YEARS)

1802 BC, *1846 BC (U)*

13. ISAAC BUILDS AN ALTAR AT BEER-SHEBA

1871 BC (U)

14. RACHEL BORN

1797 BC

15. ISAAC AND ABIMELEK TREATY

16. JACOB GETS ISAAC'S BLESSING

1789 BC, 1760 BC (U)

17. JACOB AND ESAU BOTH LEAVE TEMPORARILY

1789 BC

18. ISHMAEL DIES (137 YEARS)

1789 BC, *1773 BC (U)*

19. ESAU HAS FIRST SON, ELIPHAZ BORN

1787 BC

20. JACOB RETURNS TO HEBRON

1775 BC

21. JACOB FLEES TO LABAN

1775 BC, 1759 BC (U)

22. SEVEN YEARS LABOR FOR RACHEL

1775-1768 BC

23. EBER DIES (464 YEARS)

1773 BC

24. LABAN'S SON BEOR BORN

(LINEAGE OF JANNES, JAMBRES, AND BALAAM)

1771 BC

25. ESAU'S FIRST WIFE JUDITH DIES

1770 BC

26. JACOB MARRIES LEAH

1768 BC

27. ESAU HAS THREE MORE CHILDREN

28. JACOB'S CHILDREN - THE TWELVE TRIBES OF ISRAEL BORN

1768 BC, 1758 BC (U)

29. HAMMURABI EXTENDS THE BABYLONIAN KINGDOM, MARI TO GULF OF PERSIA

30. JACOB'S FLOCKS INCREASE

1739 BC (U)

31. JACOB FLEES FROM LABAN

1755 BC, *1739 BC (U)*

32. JACOB PREPARES TO MEET ESAU

33. THE JOURNEY CONTINUES

1754 BC

34. DINAH AND THE SHECHEMITES

35. JACOB RETURNS TO BETHEL

1753 BC

36. BACK TO HEBRON

1747 BC

D. JOSEPH

1. AT AGE SEVENTEEN

1744 BC, *1728 BC (U)*

2. JOSEPH PROSPERS IN EGYPT

3. JOSEPH AND POTIPHAR'S WIFE

4. JOSEPH IMPRISONED

1743 BC, 1717 BC (U)

5. ISRAEL'S GENEALOGIES (3RD GEN FROM JACOB)

c. 1737 BC

      6. JUDAH'S HOUSE

      7. THE CUPBEARER AND THE BAKER

1734 BC

      8. JUDAH AND TAMAR

      9. ISRAEL'S GENEALOGIES - PEREZ BORN TO TAMAR (40TH GEN TO JESUS)

1733 BC

      10. THE DREAMS OF THE CUPBEARER AND BAKER INTERPRETED

1733 BC

      11. ISAAC DIES (180 YEARS)

1732 BC, *1716 BC (U)*

      12. JOSEPH BECOMES SECOND IN COMMAND OF EGYPT

1731 BC, *1715 BC (U)*

      13. SEVEN PROSPEROUS YEARS

1731-1724 BC, *1715-1708 BC (U)*

      14. JOSEPH'S TWO SONS BORN

1727 BC

      15. THE SEVEN PROSPEROUS YEARS END

1724 BC

      16. SEVEN FAMINE YEARS

1724-1717 BC, *1708-1701 BC (U)*

      17. ISRAEL'S GENEALOGIES - HEZRON BORN (39TH GEN TO JESUS)

      18. JACOB GOES TO EGYPT

1722 BC

      19. JOSEPH AND THE FAMINE

1721 BC, *1702 BC (U)*

      20. JACOB'S BLESSING OF MANASSEH AND EPHRAIM

1689 BC (U)

      21. JACOB'S LAST DAYS

1705 BC

      22. JACOB DIES (147 YEARS)

1705 BC, *1689 BC (U)*

      23. ESAU DIES (147 YEARS)

1705 BC

      24. JOSEPH REASSURES HIS BROTHERS

      25. SONS OF ESAU GAIN FULL POSSESSION OF EDOM AFTER ESAU'S DEATH

      26. BELA FIRST KING OF EDOM (RULES 30 YEARS)

1702 BC

  E. JOB

1. PROLOGUE - THE TRIAL OF JOB BEGINS

c. 1697 BC, 1635 BC (U)

    2. FIRST SET OF DISSERTATIONS

    3. SECOND SET OF DISSERTATIONS

    4. THIRD SET OF DISSERTATIONS

    5. ELIHU'S SPEECH (DESCENDANT OF NAHOR II, ABRAHAM'S BROTHER)

    6. THE LORD SPEAKS

    7. PROSPERITY AFTER REPENTANCE

    8. ISRAEL'S GENEALOGIES - RAM BORN (38TH GEN TO JESUS)

    9. JOBAB SECOND KING OF EDOM (RULES 10 YEARS)

1672 BC

    10. BALAAM BORN - SON OF BEOR (BROTHER OF BELA)

1662 BC

    11. HUSHAM THIRD KING OF EDOM (RULES 20 YEARS)

1662 BC

    12. TRIBE OF EPHRAIM GENEALOGY

    13. JOSEPH'S FINAL DAYS

1651 BC

    14. JOSEPH DIES (110 YEARS)

1651 BC, *1635 BC (U)*

F. EGYPTIANS RULE OVER ISRAELITES

1651-1507 BC, *1635-1491 BC (U)*

    1. ZEBULUN DIES (114 YEARS)

1648 BC

    2. SIMEON DIES (120 YEARS)

1647 BC

    3. TRIBE OF EPHRAIM GENEALOGY

    4. ZEPHO (ESAU'S GRANDSON, BROTHER OF AMALEK)

1643 BC

    5. REUBEN DIES (125 YEARS)

1643 BC

    6. DAN DIES (123 YEARS)

1642 BC

    7. HADAD FOURTH KING OF EDOM (RULES 35 YEARS)

1642 BC

G. HEBREW PEOPLE GREATLY MULTIPLY

    1. ISRAEL'S NUMBERS DISTURB PHARAOH

    2. ISRAEL'S IDOLATRY BEGINS

    3. ICE MELTING CAUSES OCEANS TO RISE (ENDING ICE AGE)

H. THE ISRAELITE OPPRESSION - EGYPTIAN SLAVERY BEGINS

    1. NEW PHARAOH OVER EGYPT (SENUSRET III)

1620 BC

    2. THE HEBREWS DEFEAT ZEPHO KING OF KITTIM

WORLD SUPREMACY BELONGS TO EGYPT

    3. THE EGYPTIANS BECOME FEARFUL OF THE HEBREWS

    4. ISRAEL'S GENEALOGIES - AMMINADAB BORN (37TH GEN TO JESUS)

    5. KOHATH DIES, SON OF LEVI (133 YEARS)

    6. SAMLAH FIFTH KING OF EDOM (RULES 18 YEARS)

1607 BC

    7. PHARAOH (SENUSRET III) INCREASES OPPRESSION

1597 BC

I. MOSES

    1. MOSES' PARENTS MARRY (AMRAM'S AUNT)

1596 BC

    2. ZEPHO DIES (ESAU'S GRANDSON, BROTHER OF AMALEK)

1593 BC

    3. ALL BABY BOYS MUST DIE

1592 BC

    4. AARON BORN

1591 BC

    5. SHAUL SIXTH KING OF EDOM (RULES 40 YEARS)

1589 BC

    6. MOSES BORN

1587 BC, *1571 BC (U)*

    7. MOSES DISCOVERED BY PHARAOH'S DAUGHTER BITHIAH

    8. MOSES GROWS IN WISDOM AND STATURE

    9. THE HEBREW'S IDOLATRY IN EGYPT INCREASES

    10. JOB DIES

c. 1557 BC

    11. AARON MARRIES

    12. CECROPS FOUNDS ATHENS, TRANSPORTS COLONY FROM SAIS (EGYPT)

1556 BC (U)

13. BAAL-HANAN SEVENTH KING OF EDOM (RULES 38 YEARS)

1549 BC

14. ISRAEL'S GENEALOGIES - JOSHUA BORN

1549 BC

15. BABYLON DESTROYED, ARABIANS RULE

1538 BC (U)

16. MOSES KILLS EGYPTIAN AND LEAVES EGYPT

1547 BC, *1531 BC (U)*

17. LATINUS RULES KITTIM (ROME)

1543 BC

18. ISRAEL'S GENEALOGIES - NAHSHON BORN (36TH GEN TO JESUS)

1521 BC, ***1531 BC (U)***

19. MOSES IN MIDIAN

20. PHARAOH (SENUSRET III) DIES

1516 BC

21. HADAD II EIGHTH KING OF EDOM (RULES 48 YEARS)

1511 BC

22. MOSES MARRIES ZIPPORAH

1511 BC

J. MOSES' CALLING

1. AARON TOLD TO MEET MOSES IN THE DESERT
2. MOSES AND THE BURNING BUSH AT MOUNT SINAI

1507 BC, *1491 BC (U)*

3. SIGNS FOR MOSES
4. MOSES OBEYS

K. MOSES RETURNS TO EGYPT TO SET GOD'S PEOPLE FREE

1. THE LORD COMMANDS MOSES
2. THE PEOPLE BELIEVE GOD
3. MOSES CONFRONTS PHARAOH (AHMOSE I)

1507 BC

4. THE TEN PLAGUES

1507 BC, *1491 BC (U)*

L. THE EXODUS

1. 480 YEARS TO THE TEMPLE

1507-1027 BC, *1491-1012 BC (U)*

2. THE FIRST BORN OF EGYPT DIE

1507 BC, *1491 BC (U)*

       3. EGYPTIANS URGE HEBREWS TO LEAVE

       4. HEBREWS SAW ALL THE MIRACLES TO KNOW GOD

       5. THE DELIVERANCE OF ISRAEL

1507 BC

       6. THE JOURNEY INTO THE WILDERNESS BEGINS

       7. THE CAMP AT SUKKOTH (FEAST OF UNLEAVENED BREAD)

       8. THEY TURN SOUTH TO ETHAM

       9. THE PILLAR OF FIRE FOR NIGHT AND CLOUD FOR DAY PROVIDED

       10. LEAVE ETHAM TURNING TOWARD PI HAHIROTH

       11. PHARAOH'S HEART HARDENS AGAIN AND PURSUES

       12. CROSSING THE RED SEA AT NIGHT (EAST ARM - GULF OF AQABA)

1491 BC (U)

M. FROM THE RED SEA TO MOUNT SINAI

1507 BC

       1. THE SONG OF MOSES AND MIRIAM

       2. THE WATERS OF MARAH AND ELIM

       3. MANNA AND QUAIL

1507 BC, *1491 BC (U)*

       4. WATER FROM THE ROCK

       5. THE AMALEKITES DEFEATED

       6. JETHRO VISITS MOSES

       7. ONTO MOUNT SINAI (MIDIAN - MODERN SAUDI ARABIA)

1507 BC

A. THE LAW GIVEN AT MOUNT SINAI (HOREB)
(FIFTH DISPENSATION - LAW)

(FIFTH COVENANT - MOSAIC)

    1. REVELATION FOR THE LAW DISPENSATION

1507 BC, *1491 BC (U)*

    2. MOSES RETURNS TO THE MOUNTAIN (FOURTH CLIMB)

    3. MOSES TRAVELS AGAIN TO THE MOUNTAIN (FIFTH CLIMB - FIRST 40 DAYS)

    4. ISRAEL'S IDOLATROUS SIN

1491 BC (U)

    5. MOSES RETURNS TO THE MOUNTAIN (SEVENTH CLIMB - THIRD 40 DAYS)

    6. THE RADIANT FACE OF MOSES

    7. THE TABERNACLE CONSTRUCTION

    8. THE ORDINATION OF AARON AND HIS SONS

1506 BC, *1490 BC (U)*

    9. LEVITE PRIESTHOOD DUTIES AND NUMBERING

    10. THE SANCTIFICATION OF THE LEVITES

    11. THE PURITY OF THE CAMP

    12. TABERNACLE FINISHED

1506 BC, *1490 BC (U)*

    13. THE DEATH OF NADAB AND ABIHU

1506 BC

    14. THE DAY OF ATONEMENT PROCEDURES

    15. PRIESTHOOD PROCEDURES

    16. OFFERINGS AT THE DEDICATION OF THE TABERNACLE (12 DAYS)

1506 BC

    17. THE SECOND PASSOVER

1506 BC, *1490 BC (U)*

    18. LAWS WRITTEN

    19. THE CENSUS (603,550)

1506 BC, *1490 BC (U)*

    20. CAPITAL PUNISHMENT

    21. THE SILVER TRUMPETS

B. THE ISRAELITES LEAVE SINAI

    1. THE COMMAND TO LEAVE HOREB

1506 BC, *1490 BC (U)*

    2. GOD'S LEADING, ISRAEL FOLLOWS THE CLOUD

3. THE TRIBES ARRANGED BY DIVISIONS

4. MOSES' FATHER-IN-LAW REFUSES TO GO

5. THE JOURNEY BEGINS TO THE DESERT OF PARAN

1506 BC

6. THE JOURNEY TO HAZEROTH

7. THE JOURNEY TO KADESH BARNEA

1490 BC (U)

C. THE JOURNEY FROM KADESH BARNEA TO JORDAN CROSSING

1506-1468 BC, *1490-1452 BC (U)*

1. MOSES GIVES GOD'S COMMAND TO POSSESS THE LAND

1506 BC, *1490 BC (U)*

2. FIRST DAY OF ATONEMENT OBSERVED

1506 BC

3. THE RETURN TO THE WILDERNESS

1505 BC, *1490 BC (U)*

4. THE WANDERING IN THE WILDERNESS FOR 40 YEARS TOTAL

1507-1467 BC, *1491-1451 BC (U)*

5. SIHON THE AMORITE VICTORY OVER MOAB

1471 BC

6. THE KINGDOM OF TYRE FOUNDED (CITY FOUNDED MUCH EARLIER)

1455 BC (U)

7. THE JOURNEY TO MOAB

1468 BC, *1452 BC (U)*

8. THE JOURNEY TO THE JORDAN

1467 BC, *1452 (U)*

9. THE CAMP EAST OF THE JORDAN

10. LAWS GIVEN AT MOUNT PISGAH

11. VENGEANCE ON THE MIDIANITES

12. ISRAEL'S LAW REVIEWED FOR THE NEXT GENERATION

1468 BC, *1451 BC (U)*

(SIXTH COVENANT - PALESTINIAN)

1467 BC

13. MOSES' LAST WORDS

1467 BC

14. MOSES DIES (120 YEARS)

1467 BC, *1451 BC (U)*

15. JOSHUA IS NOW THE NEW LEADER OF ISRAEL

16. THE LORD DRIVES OUT THE NATIONS

VII. CONQUEST - THE LAND OF CANAAN: *1467-605 BC*

A. POSSESSING THE LAND OF CANAAN

    1. PREPARATION FOR CONQUEST

1467 BC, *1451 BC (U)*

    2. CROSSING THE JORDAN

1467 BC, *1451 BC (U)*

    3. THE INVASION OF CANAAN - CENTRAL CAMPAIGN

1467 BC

    4. AI DESTROYED

    5. THE COVENANT RENEWED AT MOUNT EBAL

    6. THE GIBEONITE DECEPTION (HIVITES)

    7. THE ANGEL OF THE LORD AT BOKIM

    8. SOUTHERN CAMPAIGN

    9. NORTHERN KINGS DEFEATED

    10. VICTORY BRINGS REST TO ISRAEL

    11. LIST OF DEFEATED KINGS

    12. LAND STILL TO BE TAKEN

    13. DIVISION FOR TRIBES WEST OF THE JORDON RIVER BEGINS

1462 BC, *1445 BC (U)*

    14. THE TABERNACLE SETUP AT SHILOH

    15. DIVISION OF THE REST OF THE LAND

    16. CITY ALLOCATION

    17. THE LAND'S FIRST SABBATH REST

    18. EASTERN TRIBES RETURN HOME

    19. LATINUS II RULES KITTIM (ROME)

1454-1404 BC

    20. JOSHUA'S FAREWELL TO THE LEADERS

1441 BC

    21. THE COVENANT RENEWED AT SHECHEM

    22. JOSEPH'S BONES BURIED AT SHECHEM

    23. JOSHUA DIES (110 YEARS)

1439 BC

    24. ELEAZAR DIES (LAW SEALED UP FOR 400 YEARS UNTIL ZADOK THE PRIEST)

B. THE PERIOD OF THE JUDGES

    1. ISRAEL FIGHTS THE REMAINING CANAANITES

    2. CANAANITE TRIBES NOT COMPLETELY DRIVEN OUT

    3. PHINEHAS OVERSEES THE GATEKEEPERS

4. THE ELDERS SERVE THE LORD AFTER JOSHUA'S DEATH

1423 BC

    5. NEW GENERATION THAT DOES NOT KNOW THE LORD

1413 BC (U)

    6. THE CYCLE SUMMARIZED - APOSTASY, OPPRESSION, REPENTANCE, DELIVERANCE

    7. EXAMPLES OF APOSTASY

    8. CIVIL WAR - ISRAELITES FIGHT THE BENJAMITES

    9. THE FIRST OPPRESSION FROM ARAM (MESOPOTAMIA)

1423-1415 BC, *1413-1405 BC (U)*

    10. ISRAEL'S GENEALOGIES - CALEB'S (THE SPY) GRANDSON

    11. OTHNIEL

1415-1375 BC, *1405-1343 BC (U)*

    12. SECOND APOSTASY AND OPPRESSION BY MOAB (18 YEARS)

1393-1375 BC, *1343-1325 BC (U)*

    13. EHUD

1375-1295 BC, *1325-1285 BC (U)*

    14. ISRAEL'S GENEALOGIES - BOAZ BORN (34TH GEN TO JESUS)

    15. SHAMGAR

    16. THIRD APOSTASY AND OPPRESSION BY CANAANITES (20 YEARS)

1315-1295 BC, *1305-1285 BC (U)*

    17. ISRAEL'S GENEALOGIES - SAMUEL'S GRANDFATHER

    18. DEBORAH AND BARAK

1295-1255 BC, *1285-1245 BC (U)*

    19. FOURTH APOSTASY AND OPPRESSION BY MIDIANITES (SEVEN YEARS)

1262-1255 BC, *1252-1245 BC (U)*

    20. GIDEON (JERUB-BAAL)

1255-1215 BC, *1245-1205 BC (U)*

    21. GIDEON DEFEATS THE MIDIANITES

1215-1173 BC (U)

    22. GIDEON DIES

1215 BC, *1205 BC (U)*

    23. THE FIFTH APOSTASY

    24. ABIMELEK

1215-1212 BC, *1236-1233 BC (U)*

    25. TOLA

1212-1189 BC, *1223-1210 BC (U)*

    26. BOOK OF RUTH

    27. ISRAEL'S GENEALOGIES - OBED BORN (33RD GEN TO JESUS)

    28. JAIR

1189-1167 BC, *1210-1188 BC (U)*

        29. PHILISTINES DEFEATED BY EGYPT

        30. TROY DESTROYED BY GREEKS

1184 BC (U)

        31. ELI - EIGHTH JUDGE (CO JUDGES 40 YEARS)

1157-1117 BC (U)

        32. JEPHTHAH'S EARLY YEARS

        33. SAMSON'S DANITE PARENTS

1156 BC (U)

        34. SIXTH APOSTASY AND OPPRESSION (AMMONITES AND PHILISTINES)

1185-1167 BC, *1206-1188 BC (U)*

        35. JEPHTHAH

1167-1161 BC, *1188-1182 BC (U)*

        36. IBZAN

1161-1154 BC, *1182-1175 BC (U)*

        37. PHILISTINES OPPRESSION FROM THE WEST (40 YEARS)

1156-1116 BC, *1156-1116 BC (U)*

        38. SAMUEL'S EPHRAIMITE PARENTS

        39. ISRAEL'S GENEALOGIES - JESSE BORN (32ND GEN TO JESUS)

        40. SAMUEL'S DEDICATION

        41. ELON

1154-1144 BC, *1175-1165 BC (U)*

        42. ABDON

1144-1136 BC, *1165-1157 BC (U)*

        43. SAMSON

1136-1116 BC, *1137-1117 BC (U)*

        44. ELI'S WICKED SONS

        45. SAMUEL GROWS IN STATURE WITH THE LORD AND PEOPLE

        46. THE LORD CALLS SAMUEL

        47. PROPHECY AGAINST THE HOUSE OF ELI

        48. PHILISTINES OPPRESSION CONTINUES

        49. SAMUEL'S JUDGESHIP

        50. SAMUEL SUBDUES THE PHILISTINES AT MIZPAH

1113 BC (U)

    C. THE UNITED KINGDOM

1110-990 BC, *1095-975 BC (U)*

        1. SAUL REIGNS

1110-1070 BC, *1095-1055 BC (U)*

        2. DAVID REIGNS

1070-1030 BC, *1055-1015 BC (U)*

WORLD SUPREMACY BELONGS TO ISRAEL

3. SOLOMON REIGNS

1030-990 BC, *1015-975 BC (U)*

4. THE BOOK OF THE SONG OF SOLOMON

992 BC (U)

5. THE BOOK OF PROVERBS

6. BOOK OF ECCLESIASTES

990 BC, *975 BC (U)*

D. THE DIVIDED KINGDOM

JUDAH (SOUTHERN KINGDOM) - ISRAEL (NORTHERN KINGDOM)

990-605 BC, *975-607 BC (U)*

1. JUDAH - REHOBOAM - 17 YEAR EVIL REIGN

(41 YEARS OLD)

990-973 BC, *975-958 BC (U)*

2. ISRAEL - JEROBOAM I - 22 YEAR EVIL REIGN

990-968 BC, *975-953 BC (U)*

3. JUDAH - ABIJAH - 3 YEAR EVIL REIGN

972-969 BC, *958-955 BC (U)*

4. JUDAH - ASA - 41 YEAR GOOD REIGN

970-929 BC, *955-914 BC (U)*

5. ISRAEL - NADAB - TWO YEAR EVIL REIGN (DUEL WITH JEROBOAM)

969-967 BC, *955-953 BC (U)*

6. ISRAEL - BAASHA - 24 YEAR EVIL REIGN

967-944 BC, *953-930 BC (U)*

7. ISRAEL - ELAH - TWO YEAR EVIL REIGN

944-943 BC, *930-929 BC (U)*

8. ISRAEL - ZIMRI - SEVEN DAY EVIL REIGN

943 BC, *929 BC (U)*

9. ISRAEL - OMRI - 12 YEAR EVIL REIGN

943-931 BC, *929-918 BC (U)*

10. ISRAEL - AHAB - 22 YEARS EVIL REIGN

932-910 BC, *918-896 BC (U)*

11. JUDAH - JEHOSHAPHAT - 25 YEAR GOOD REIGN

(35 YEARS OLD)

928-903 BC, *914-889 BC (U)*

12. ISRAEL - AHAZIAH - TWO YEAR EVIL REIGN

911-909 BC, *896-894 BC (U)*

13. ISRAEL - JORAM - 12 YEAR EVIL REIGN

910-898 BC, *896-884 BC (U)*

14. JUDAH - JEHORAM - EIGHT YEAR EVIL REIGN

(32 YEARS OLD)

905-897 BC, *889-885 BC (U)*

15. JUDAH - AHAZIAH (AZARIAH) - ONE YEAR EVIL REIGN

(22 YEARS OLD)

898-897 BC, *885-884 BC (U)*

16. JUDAH - ATHALIAH - SIX YEAR EVIL REIGN

897-891 BC, *884-878 BC (U)*

17. ISRAEL - JEHU - 28 YEAR GOOD AND EVIL REIGN

898-870 BC, *884-856 BC (U)*

18. JUDAH - JOASH - 40 YEAR GOOD AND EVIL REIGN

(7 YEARS OLD)

891-851 BC, *878-839 BC (U)*

19. ISRAEL - JEHOAHAZ - 17 YEAR EVIL REIGN

868-851 BC, *856-839 BC (U)*

20. ISRAEL - JEHOASH - 16 YEAR EVIL REIGN

854-838 BC, *841-825 BC (U)*

21. JUDAH - AMAZIAH - 29 YEAR GOOD REIGN

(25 YEARS OLD)

852-823 BC, *839-810 BC (U)*

22. ISRAEL - JEROBOAM II - 41 YEAR EVIL REIGN

(28 YEARS OLD)

837-796 BC, *825-784 BC (U)*

23. JUDAH - UZZIAH (AZARIAH) - 52 YEAR GOOD REIGN

(16 YEARS OLD)

810-758 BC, *810-758 BC (U)*

24. ISRAEL - ZECHARIAH - SIX MONTH EVIL REIGN

772-772 BC, *773 BC (U)*

25. ISRAEL - SHALLUM - ONE MONTH EVIL REIGN

771 BC, *773 BC (U)*

26. ISRAEL - MENAHEM - 10 YEAR EVIL REIGN

771-761 BC, *771-761 BC (U)*

27. ISRAEL - PEKAHIAH - TWO YEAR EVIL REIGN

760-758 BC, *761-759 BC (U)*

28. JUDAH - JOTHAM - 16 YEAR GOOD REIGN

(25 YEARS OLD)

756-740 BC, *759-742 BC (U)*

WORLD SUPREMACY BELONGS TO ASSYRIA
747-626 BC (U)

          29. ISRAEL - PEKAH - 20 YEAR EVIL REIGN

758-738 BC, *758-739 BC (U)*

          30. JUDAH - AHAZ - 16 YEARS EVIL REIGN

        (20 YEARS OLD)

740-724 BC, *742-726 BC (U)*

          31. JUDAH - HEZEKIAH - 29 YEAR GOOD REIGN

        (25 YEARS OLD)

725-696 BC, *727-698 BC (U)*

          32. ISRAEL - HOSHEA - NINE YEAR EVIL REIGN

728-719 BC, *730-721 BC (U)*

          E. JUDAH DURING THE ASSYRIAN CAPTIVITY OF ISRAEL

          1. HEZEKIAH'S REIGN CONTINUES

718 BC (U)

          2. MANASSEH - 55 YEAR EVIL REIGN

        (12 YEARS OLD)

696-641 BC, *698-643 BC (U)*

          3. AMON - TWO YEAR EVIL REIGN (22 YEARS OLD)

641-639 BC, *643-641 BC (U)*

          4. JOSIAH - 31 YEAR GOOD REIGN (8 YEARS OLD)

639-608 BC, *641-610 BC (U)*

WORLD SUPREMACY BELONGS TO BABYLON
(DANIEL'S FIRST WORLD EMPIRE OF DAN 7:17)
626-538 (U)

          5. JEHOAHAZ (SHALLUM) - THREE MONTH EVIL REIGN

        (23 YEARS OLD - JOSIAH'S SON)

608 BC, *610 BC (U)*

          6. JEHOIAKIM - 11 YEAR EVIL REIGN

        (25 YEARS OLD - JOSIAH'S SECOND SON)

608-597 BC, *610-599 BC (U)*

          7. NEBUCHADNEZZAR REIGNS AS KING OF BABYLON

605-560 BC, *607-562 BC (U)*

VIII. CAPTIVITY - DEPORTATION TO BABYLON: *605-3 BC*

A. DEPORTATIONS - 70 YEARS OF CAPTIVITY BEGINS

1. JEHOIAKIM ATTACKED (JERUSALEM BESIEGED FIRST TIME BY BABYLON)

2. JEHOIAKIM CAPTURED, REMAINS KING AS VASSAL TO NEBUCHADNEZZAR

605-536 BC, *607-537 BC (U)*

3. A FAST PROCLAIMED

603 BC, *606 BC (U)*

4. JEHOIAKIM BURNS JEREMIAH'S SCROLL

605 BC (U)

5. NEBUCHADNEZZAR'S TERRITORY INCREASES

605 BC (U)

6. NABOPOLASSAR DIES

605 BC (U)

7. DANIEL'S TRAINING IN BABYLON

604 BC (U)

8. NEBUCHADNEZZAR'S DREAM - THE GREAT STATUE

603 BC, *604 BC (U)*

9. JEREMIAH'S PROPHECIES CONTINUE IN JERUSALEM

10. JEREMIAH AND PASHHUR

11. JEHOIAKIM REBELS AGAINST NEBUCHADNEZZAR

602 BC, *604 BC (U)*

12. JEHOIAKIM SURROUNDED BY ENEMIES

599 BC, *600 BC (U)*

13. DARIUS THE MEDE (CYAXARES) BORN

600 BC (U)

14. JEHOIAKIM DIES

597 BC, *599 BC (U)*

15. JEHOIACHIN (JECONIAH) - THREE MONTH EVIL REIGN
(18 YEARS OLD - JOSIAH'S GRANDSON)

597 BC, *599 BC (U)*

16. CYRUS OF PERSIA BORN

599 BC (U)

17. ZEDEKIAH (MATTANIAH) - 11 YEAR EVIL REIGN
(21 YEARS OLD - JOSIAH'S SON)

597-586 BC, *599-588 BC (U)*

18. EZEKIEL'S PROPHECIES FROM BABYLON

592 BC

19. NEBUCHADNEZZAR APPROACHES JERUSALEM

591 BC (U)

B. THE FALL OF JERUSALEM
    1. JERUSALEM UNDER SIEGE AGAIN

588-586 BC, *590-588 BC (U)*
    2. JEREMIAH'S PROPHECIES CONTINUE

588 BC, *590 BC (U)*
    3. PHARAOH HOPHRA (APRIES) ENGAGES AGAINST NEBUCHADNEZZAR

590 BC (U)
    4. NEBUCHADNEZZAR RETURNS TO JERUSALEM

589 BC (U)
    5. PROPHECIES AGAINST ISRAEL'S NEIGHBORS

586 BC, *588 BC (U)*
    6. FAMINE PREVAILS

586 BC, *588 BC (U)*
    7. JERUSALEM FALLS

586 BC, *588 BC (U)*
    8. TEMPLE DESTROYED

586 BC, *588 BC (U)*
    9. THE FIFTH DEPORTATION

588 BC (U)
    10. SABBATH REST FOR THE LAND
    11. POOREST LEFT BEHIND
    12. GEDALIAH THE GOVERNOR OF JUDAH

588 BC (U)
    13. JEREMIAH TREATED WELL BY BABYLONIANS

588 BC (U)
    14. LAMENTATIONS OVER JERUSALEM
    15. SCATTERED JEWS RETURN TO JUDAH

588 BC (U)
    16. GEDALIAH ASSASSINATED

588 BC (U)
    17. ISHMAEL FLEES TO AMMONITES
    18. FLIGHT TO EGYPT

588 BC (U)
    19. JERUSALEM'S FALL EXPLAINED

586 BC, *587 BC (U)*
    20. PROPHECIES AGAINST EGYPT GIVEN

585 BC, *587 BC (U)*

21. JEREMIAH'S PROPHECY IN EGYPT

22. OBADIAH'S VISION OF EDOM'S GREAT SIN

587 BC (U)

23. MAINLAND TYRE BESIEGED

585-572 BC (U)

24. NEBUCHADNEZZAR PILLAGES AMMON, MOAB, AND EDOM

585-572 BC (U)

25. THE PROMISED LAND DESOLATE

26. NEBUCHADNEZZAR'S IMAGE OF GOLD

27. EZEKIEL'S WATCHMAN

28. A PROPHECY AGAINST GOG - VISION OF WORLD WAR III

29. THE NEW TEMPLE AREA - VISION OF MILLENNIAL REIGN

572 BC, *575 BC (U)*

30. A LAMENT FOR EGYPT

570 BC, *573 BC (U)*

C. BABYLON AT ITS HEIGHT

1. MAINLAND TYRE FINALLY SURRENDERS TO NEBUCHADNEZZAR

572 BC (U)

2. NEBUCHADNEZZAR'S INVASIONS

571 BC (U)

3. NEBUCHADNEZZAR'S PROCLAMATION

570 BC (U)

4. NEBUCHADNEZZAR'S SECOND DREAM

570 BC (U)

5. NEBUCHADNEZZAR BUILDS THE HANGING GARDENS FOR HIS WIFE

570 BC (U)

6. THE DREAM IS FULFILLED

570-563 BC (U)

7. NEBUCHADNEZZAR REPENTS

563 BC (U)

8. NEBUCHADNEZZAR DIES

560 BC, *562-560 BC (U)*

9. JEHOIACHIN RELEASED FROM PRISON

560 BC, *562 BC (U)*

10. ISRAEL'S GENEALOGIES - SHEALTIEL BORN (13TH GEN TO JESUS)

11. JEHOIACHIN DIES - ISRAEL WITHOUT A KING UNTIL JESUS RETURNS

(2,600 YEARS APX)

560 BC (U)

12. JEREMIAH DIES

13. AWEL-MARDUK KILLED

560-556 BC (U)

14. THE MEDES AND PERSIANS UNITE

559 BC (U)

15. CYRUS REIGNS IN PERSIA

559-529 BC (U)

16. ISRAEL'S LIGHT GROWS DIM, BUT THEY REPENT AND TURN BACK TO THE LORD

D. BIRTH OF THE WORLD'S PHILOSOPHIES (HUMANISM)

1. BUDDHA BORN IN INDIA

2. CONFUCIUS BORN IN CHINA

3. ZOROASTRIANISM ROOTS IN IRAN

4. JAINISM ROOTS IN INDIA

5. GREEK PHILOSOPHY STARTS

6. LABOROSOARCHODUS (LABASHI-MARDUK) REIGNS IN BABYLON

556 BC (U)

7. NABONIDUS (AWEL-MARDUK'S SON) REIGNS IN BABYLON

555-538 BC (U)

8. DANIEL'S DREAM OF THE FOUR BEASTS

(DANIEL'S FOUR WORLD EMPIRES)

555 BC (U)

9. PSALMS OF THE CAPTIVITY

10. DANIEL'S VISION OF A RAM AND A GOAT

(KINGS OF MEDO-PERSIA AND GREECE)

553 BC (U)

11. ISRAEL'S GENEALOGIES - ZERUBBABEL BORN (12TH GEN TO JESUS)

12. THE MEDES AND PERSIANS ARISE

546 BC (U)

13. THE GREAT BANQUET

538 BC (U)

E. MEDES AND PERSIANS DEFEAT BABYLON
(DANIEL'S SECOND WORLD EMPIRE FOR DAN 7:17)

1. KINGDOM CHARACTERISTICS

2. DARIUS THE MEDE (CYAXARES) CONQUERS

538 BC (U)

WORLD SUPREMACY BELONGS TO MEDO-PERSIA

538-333 BC (U)

3. DARIUS THE MEDE (CYAXARES) BEGINS REIGN FROM BABYLON

538-521 BC (U)

    4. DANIEL IN THE DEN OF LIONS

538 BC (U)

    5. DANIEL'S PRAYER

538 BC (U)

    6. ISRAEL'S TIME CLOCK OF 490 YEARS (70 WEEKS OF SEVEN YEARS)

    7. CYRUS BEGINS REIGN FROM BABYLON - CYRUS HELPS THE EXILES TO RETURN

    (DARIUS' THIRD YEAR)

535 BC, *537 BC (U)*

    8. PEOPLE'S ANSWER

536 BC (U)

    9. TEMPLE TREASURES RETURNED TO SHESHBAZZAR (ZERUBBABEL)

536 BC (U)

    10. TEMPLE MATERIALS

535 BC

    11. ZERUBBABEL LEADS THE PEOPLE

536 BC (U)

    12. REBUILDING OF THE ALTAR - FOR THE FEAST OF TRUMPETS

535 BC, *536 BC (U)*

  F. REBUILDING OF THE TEMPLE

    1. THE FOUNDATION LAID

533 BC, *535 BC (U)*

    2. OPPOSITION TO REBUILDING - SAMARITAN'S HELP DECLINED

535 BC (U)

    3. DANIEL'S VISION OF A GREAT WAR

532 BC, *534 BC (U)*

    4. CYRUS SENDS EGYPTIAN CAPTIVES BACK TO EGYPT

531 BC (U)

    5. CYRUS DIES (70 YEARS)

529 BC (U)

    6. CAMBYSES II REIGNS OVER MEDO-PERSIA (TITLE OF XERXES)

529-522 BC (U)

    7. CAMBYSES II CONQUERS EGYPT (THIRD RIB OF DAN 7:5)

525 BC (U)

    8. SMERDIS RULES MEDO-PERSIA SEVEN MONTHS (TITLE OF ARTAXERXES)

522 BC (U)

    9. KING'S ANSWER COMMANDS BUILDING STOPPED

522-521 BC (U)

10. TEMPLE WORK POSTPONED

522-520 BC (U)

      11. DARIUS I REIGNS OVER MEDO-PERSIA (TITLES OF XERXES OR AHASUERUS)

522-485 BC (U)

      12. HAGGAI'S PROPHECIES

520 BC (U)

      13. WORK ON THE TEMPLE RESUMES

520 BC (U)

      14. THE PROMISE OF GLORY FOR THE NEW HOUSE

520 BC (U)

      15. ZECHARIAH'S PROPHECIES

520 BC (U)

      16. BLESSINGS FOR A DEFILED PEOPLE

520 BC (U)

      17. ZERUBBABEL THE LORD'S SIGNET RING

520 BC (U)

      18. ZECHARIAH'S EIGHT VISIONS

519 BC (U)

      19. A CROWN FOR JOSHUA (PICTURE OF THE MESSIAH CROWNED)

      20. BUILDING OPPOSITION

519 BC (U)

G. ESTER SAVES ISRAEL

      1. IDENTIFICATION OF DARIUS I (TITLE OF XERXES)

518 BC (U)

      2. BANQUET FOR OFFICIALS

518 BC (U)

      3. QUEEN VASHTI'S DISOBEDIENCE

      4. THE KING CONSULTS NOBLES

      5. QUEEN VASHTI DEPOSED

      6. NEW QUEEN SOUGHT

518 BC (U)

      7. ESTHER AT SUSA

      8. JUSTICE AND MERCY, NOT FASTING

518 BC (U)

      9. COMPLETION OF THE TEMPLE IN JERUSALEM

515 BC (U)

      10. DEDICATION OF THE TEMPLE

515 BC (U)

11. THE PASSOVER OBSERVED IN JERUSALEM

515 BC (U)

12. POTENTIAL QUEENS CONSIDERED FOR DARIUS I (TITLE OF XERXES)

515 BC (U)

13. ESTHER MADE QUEEN OF MEDO-PERSIA

515 BC (U)

14. BANQUET FOR ESTHER AT SUSA

514 BC (U)

15. MORDECAI UNCOVERS A CONSPIRACY

16. HAMAN PLOTS TO DESTROY THE ISRAELITES

510 BC (U)

17. LOTS CAST

510 BC (U)

18. THE KING'S SUPPORT GAINED BY ANIMOSITY

19. ORDER OF ISRAELITE'S ANNIHILATION

510 BC (U)

20. MORDECAI PERSUADES ESTHER TO HELP

510 BC (U)

21. ESTHER'S REQUEST TO THE KING

510 BC (U)

22. HAMAN'S RAGE AGAINST MORDECAI

23. MORDECAI HONORED

510 BC (U)

24. THE KING DINES WITH ESTHER

25. HAMAN KILLED ON HIS OWN POLE

26. THE KING'S EDICT ON BEHALF OF ISRAELITES

510 BC (U)

27. ISRAELITES CELEBRATE

28. TRIUMPH OF ISRAEL

509 BC (U)

29. PURIM CELEBRATED (LATER CELEBRATED AS ESTHER'S FAST)

509 BC (U)

30. THE GREATNESS OF MORDECAI - SECOND IN COMMAND

31. DARIUS I (XERXES) REDUCES THE NUMBER OF PROVINCES TO TWENTY

32. ZECHARIAH'S PROPHECIES CONTINUE

33. ISRAEL'S GENEALOGIES - ABIHUD BORN (11TH GEN TO JESUS)

34. REIGN OF XERXES I BEGINS (SON OF DARIUS I)

485-474 BC (U)

35. HERODOTUS BORN - "FATHER OF HISTORY" (GENTILE HISTORY)

484 BC (U)

    36. GREEKS DEFEAT PERSIA AT SALAMIS

480 BC (U)

    37. ISRAEL'S GENEALOGIES - ELIAKIM BORN (10TH GEN TO JESUS)

    38. REIGN OF ARTAXERXES I, KING OF PERSIA

472 BC, *474-425 BC (U)*

    39. THE RETURN TO JERUSALEM

465 BC, *467 BC (U)*

    40. EZRA COMES TO JERUSALEM

465 BC, *467 BC (U)*

H. DECREE TO REBUILD JERUSALEM
(TO MESSIAH'S CRUCIFIXION 483 YEARS)

    1. NEHEMIAH HEARS OF JERUSALEM'S WALLS WHILE IN BABYLON

452 BC, *455 BC (U)*

    2. NEHEMIAH'S SADNESS

451 BC, *454 BC (U)*

    3. ARTAXERXES I SENDS NEHEMIAH TO JERUSALEM

454 BC (U)

    4. ENEMIES STIRRED AGAINST THE PROJECT

    5. ARRIVED AT JERUSALEM

    6. NEHEMIAH INSPECTS JERUSALEM'S WALLS

    7. NEHEMIAH GOVERNOR OF JUDAH

451-439 BC, *454-442 BC (U)*

    8. THE DECREE TO REBUILD JERUSALEM (ISRAEL'S TIME CLOCK STARTS)

451 BC, *454 BC (U)*

    9. OPPOSITION TO REBUILDING

    10. THE COMPLETION OF THE WALL

451 BC, 454 BC (U)

    11. DEDICATION OF THE WALL

    12. JERUSALEM PROTECTED

    13. THE NEW RESIDENTS OF JERUSALEM (LOTS CAST)

454 BC (U)

    14. FEAST OF TRUMPETS

451 BC, *454 BC (U)*

    15. NEHEMIAH'S JOURNEYS

439 BC, *442 BC (U)*

    16. ISRAEL'S GENEALOGIES CONTINUE - JOSEK BORN (MARY'S LINEAGE)

    17. THE PELOPONNESIAN WAR

431-404 BC (U)
> 18. XERXES II REIGNS IN MEDO-PERSIA

425-424 BC (U)
> 19. OCHUS REIGNS IN MEDO-PERSIA (DARIUS II)

423-404 BC (U)
> 20. MALACHI'S PROPHECY

416 BC (U)
> 21. JERUSALEM FINISHED BEING REBUILT (ISRAEL'S TIME CLOCK CONTINUES)

402 BC
> 22. ISRAEL'S GENEALOGIES - AZOR BORN (9TH GEN TO JESUS)

I. THE HISTORY BETWEEN THE TESTAMENTS

402-3 BC, *416-5 BC (U)*
> 1. 400 YEARS OF SILENCE (MALACHI TO CHRIST'S BIRTH)
>
> 2. ARTAXERXES II REIGNS IN MEDO-PERSIA

404-361 BC (U)
> 3. ISRAEL'S GENEALOGIES - ZADOK BORN (8TH GEN TO JESUS)
>
> 4. ARTAXERXES III (OCHUS) REIGNS IN MEDO-PERSIA

360-338 BC (U)
> 5. PLATO DIES

348 BC (U)
> 6. ISRAEL'S GENEALOGIES CONTINUE - MAATH BORN (MARY'S LINEAGE)
>
> 7. ARTAXERXES IV (ARSES) REIGNS IN MEDO-PERSIA

338-336 BC (U)
> 8. DARIUS III REIGNS IN MEDO-PERSIA

336-330 BC (U)
> 9. THE KINGDOM OF GREECE

332 BC (U)
> 10. MEDO-PERSIAN EMPIRE FALLS

330 BC (U)
> 11. ALEXANDER THE GREAT RULES THE WORLD

330-323 BC (U)

WORLD SUPREMACY BELONGS TO GREECE

(DANIEL'S THIRD WORLD EMPIRE FOR DAN 7:17)

330-63 BC (U)
> 12. ISRAEL'S GENEALOGIES - AKIM BORN (7TH GEN TO JESUS)
>
> 13. SELEUCUS I (COMMANDER OF PTOLEMY I) PROCLAIMS HIMSELF
>   KING OF BABYLON

305-280 BC (U)
> 14. ISRAEL'S GENEALOGIES CONTINUE - ELIUD BORN (6TH GEN TO JESUS)

15. PTOLEMY II (PHILADELPHUS) GREEK KING OF THE SOUTH

285-246 BC (U)

16. ISRAEL'S GENEALOGIES CONTINUE - NAHUM BORN (MARY'S LINEAGE)

17. PTOLEMY III (EUERGETES) GREEK KING OF THE SOUTH

246-221 BC (U)

18. SELEUCUS II (CALLINICUS) GREEK KING OF THE NORTH STRIKES BACK AT PTOLEMY III

244 BC (U)

19. ATTALUS BECOMES THE SELF PROCLAIMED KING OF PERGAMUM

241 BC (U)

20. ISRAEL'S GENEALOGIES CONTINUE - AMOS BORN (MARY'S LINEAGE)

21. SELEUCUS II'S YOUNGEST SON (ANTIOCHUS III), GREEK KING OF THE NORTH

223-187 BC (U)

22. PTOLEMY IV (PHILOPATER) GREEK KING OF THE SOUTH

221-204 BC (U)

23. ISRAEL'S GENEALOGIES CONTINUE - MATTATHIAS BORN (MARY'S LINEAGE)

24. PTOLEMY V (EPIPHANES) GREEK KING OF THE SOUTH

204-180 BC (U)

25. ISRAEL'S GENEALOGIES CONTINUE - ELEAZAR BORN (5TH GEN TO JESUS)

26. SELEUCUS IV (PHILOPATER), GREEK KING OF THE NORTH

27. ISRAEL'S GENEALOGIES CONTINUE - JANNAI BORN (MARY'S LINEAGE)

187-175 BC (U)

28. PTOLEMY VI (PHILOMETOR), GREEK KING OF THE SOUTH

180-146 BC (U)

29. ANTIOCHUS IV (EPIPHANES), GREEK KING OF THE NORTH

175-164 BC (U)

30. PTOLEMY VI (PHILOMETOR) DIES, PTOLEMY VII (PHYSCON) SOLE RULE OF SOUTH

146-117 BC (U)

31. ISRAEL'S GENEALOGIES CONTINUE - MATTHAN BORN (4TH GEN TO JESUS)

32. PARTHIAN KINGDOM

141 BC (U)

33. ISRAEL'S GENEALOGIES CONTINUE - LEVI BORN (MARY'S LINEAGE)
34. PTOLEMY VIII, IX (LATHURUS/ALEXANDER) AND CLEOPATRA III, GREEK RULERS OF THE SOUTH

117-81 BC (U)

35. ISRAEL'S GENEALOGIES CONTINUE - JACOB BORN (3RD GEN TO JESUS)

36. PTOLEMY X AND XI (ALEXANDER II, AULETES), GREEK KINGS OF THE SOUTH

81-55 BC (U)

37. ISRAEL'S GENEALOGIES CONTINUE - HELI BORN (MARY'S LINEAGE)

38. POMPEY OF ROME MAKES HYRCANUS II THE HIGH PRIEST GOVERNOR OF JUDEA

64 BC (U)

      39. JULIUS CAESAR DICTATOR OF ROME

49-44 BC (U)

WORLD SUPREMACY BELONGS TO ROME

(DANIEL'S FOURTH WORLD EMPIRE FOR DAN 7:17)
49 BC-410 AD

      40. CHARACTERISTICS OF ROME

45 BC (U)

      41. JULIUS CAESAR MURDERED, OCTAVIUS RULES ROME

44 BC-14 AD (U)

      42. OCTAVIUS PRONOUNCED CAESAR AUGUSTUS BY THE SENATE

27 BC - 14 AD (U)

      43. ISRAEL'S GENEALOGIES CONTINUE - JOSEPH BORN (2ND GEN TO JESUS)

      44. HEROD THE GREAT BEGINS EXPANDING THE TEMPLE IN JERUSALEM

17 BC, *17 BC (U)*

IX. CHRIST - THE MESSIAH: *3 BC-33 AD*

A. EVENTS LEADING TO CHRIST'S BIRTH
1. THE BEGINNING OF THE GOSPELS
2. THE BIRTH OF JOHN THE BAPTIST FORETOLD

4 BC, 6 BC (U)

3. THE BIRTH OF JESUS FORETOLD

4 BC, 5 BC (U)

4. MARY VISITS ELIZABETH
5. MARY'S SONG
6. JOHN THE BAPTIST BORN

3 BC, 5 BC (U)

7. JESUS CHRIST ANNOUNCED TO JOSEPH BY AN ANGEL

B. BIRTH AND CHILDHOOD OF JESUS CHRIST - FIRST COMING
1. JESUS CHRIST BORN

3 BC, 5 BC (U)

2. THE SHEPHERDS AND THE ANGELS
3. JESUS IS CIRCUMCISED AND OFFICIALLY NAMED

3 BC, 4 BC (U)

4. JESUS PRESENTED IN THE TEMPLE

3 BC, 4 BC (U)

5. VISIT OF THE MAGI

4 BC (U)

6. ESCAPE TO EGYPT

3 BC (U)

7. RETURN TO NAZARETH

4 BC (U)

8. CHRIST'S CHILDHOOD AT NAZARETH
9. JOHN THE BAPTIST GROWS UP
10. CHRIST CELEBRATES PASSOVER AT JERUSALEM

10 AD, 8 AD (U)

11. CHRIST AT NAZARETH AS A CARPENTER
12. PAUL (SAUL) BORN
13. TIBERIUS CAESAR AUGUSTUS RULES THE ROMAN EMPIRE

14 AD - 37 AD (U)

C. JOHN THE BAPTIST PREPARES THE WAY FOR JESUS CHRIST
1. JOHN PREACHING IN THE DESERT

26 AD (U)

      2. JOHN REBUKES THE PHARISEES

      3. JOHN'S ANNOUNCEMENT OF JESUS CHRIST

D. CHRIST'S MINISTRY BEGINS

      1. BAPTISM OF JESUS

29 AD, *27 AD (U)*

      2. JESUS THE LAMB OF GOD

      3. TEMPTATION OF JESUS

29 AD, *27 AD (U)*

      4. JOHN THE BAPTIST'S MINISTRY AT BETHANY (BEYOND THE JORDAN)

      5. THE FIRST THREE DISCIPLES

      6. JESUS CALLS PHILIP AND NATHANAEL

      7. JESUS CHANGES WATER INTO WINE

30 AD (U)

      8. DOWN TO CAPERNAUM

E. CHRIST'S EARLY JUDEAN MINISTRY

      1. JESUS CLEARS THE TEMPLE

      (FIRST PASSOVER)

30 AD, *30 AD (U)*

      2. JESUS TEACHES NICODEMUS

      3. CHRIST BAPTIZES FOLLOWERS

      4. JOHN THE BAPTIST'S TESTIMONY ABOUT JESUS

      5. JOHN THE BAPTIST IMPRISONED

      6. JESUS BEGINS TO PREACH

      7. JESUS TALKS WITH A SAMARITAN WOMEN

F. CHRIST'S GALILEAN MINISTRY

      1. CHRIST RETURNS TO GALILEE

30 AD (U)

      2. FIRST TOUR

31 AD (U)

      3. HOSTILITY OF THE PHARISEES GROWS

      (SECOND PASSOVER)

31 AD, *31 AD (U)*

      4. THE SERMON ON THE MOUNT

31 AD (U)

      5. SECOND TOUR

31 AD (U)

      6. THE SEA OF GALILEE MINISTRY

31 AD (U)

      7. MIRACLES BY THE SEA OF GALILEE

31 AD (U)

      8. THIRD TOUR

31 AD (U)

      9. JESUS FEEDS THE 5,000

      (THIRD PASSOVER)

32 AD, *32 AD (U)*

      10. TRAVEL TO TYRE AND SIDON

32 AD (U)

      11. JESUS FEEDS THE 4,000

32 AD (U)

      12. TRAVEL TO CAESAREA PHILIPPI

32 AD (U)

      13. BACK IN CAPERNAUM

32 AD (U)

      14. TRAVELS TO JERUSALEM PRIVATELY

32 AD, *32 AD (U)*

      15. CHRIST RETURNS TO GALILEE

    G. CHRIST'S LAST SIX MONTHS BEFORE THE CROSS

      1. LAST DEPARTURE FROM GALILEE - SAMARITAN OPPOSITION

32 AD (U)

      2. BACK TO JERUSALEM AT THE FEAST OF DEDICATION

32 AD, *32 AD (U)*

      3. CHRIST'S LAST TOUR BEFORE THE CROSS

33 AD (U)

    H. THE PASSION WEEK

      1. CHRIST TRAVELS TO BETHANY

      (FOURTH PASSOVER)

33 AD, *33 AD (U)*

      2. JESUS ANOINTED AT BETHANY

      3. THE TRIUMPHAL ENTRY INTO JERUSALEM

33 AD, *33 AD (U)*

      4. THE FIG TREE CURSED

33 AD, *33 AD (U)*

5. JESUS CLEARS THE TEMPLE

6. THE WITHERED FIG TREE

33 AD, *33 AD (U)*

7. THE CHIEF PRIESTS QUESTION JESUS' AUTHORITY

8. JESUS RESPONDS TO THE CHIEF PRIESTS WITH MORE PARABLES

9. PHARISEES ATTEMPT TO TRAP CHRIST

10. SADDUCEES CONFRONT CHRIST

11. LAW EXPERT TEST CHRIST

12. JESUS RESPONDS TO PHARISEES AND LAW EXPERTS WITH SEVEN WOES

13. THE WIDOW'S OFFERING

33 AD, *33 AD (U)*

14. SIGNS OF THE END OF THE AGE

15. THE PLOT AGAINST JESUS

33 AD, *33 AD (U)*

16. JUDAS AGREES TO BETRAY JESUS

17. JESUS PREDICTS HIS DEATH

18. ISRAEL CONTINUES IN UNBELIEF

19. DAY OF PREPARATION FOR THE PASSOVER

33 AD, *33 AD (U)*

20. JESUS WASHES HIS DISCIPLES' FEET

33 AD, *33 AD (U)*

21. THE LORD'S SUPPER ESTABLISHED

(EIGHTH COVENANT - NEW)

22. JUDAS IDENTIFIED AS THE BETRAYER

23. ARGUMENT OVER WHO IS GREATEST

24. JESUS PREDICTS PETER'S DENIAL

25. JESUS COMFORTS HIS DISCIPLES - FAREWELL CONVERSATION

26. FAREWELL PRAYER

27. CHRIST WORSHIPS

X. CROSS - GRACE FOR THE BELIEVER: *33 AD - Present*

A. GETHSEMANE
    1. CHRIST PRAYS ON THE MOUNT OF OLIVES
    2. JUDAS LEADS ENEMIES TO CHRIST

B. THE TRIAL
    1. JESUS TAKEN TO ANNAS
33 AD, *33 AD (U)*
    2. CHRIST TAKEN TO CAIAPHAS
    3. PETER DISOWNS JESUS
    4. BEFORE THE SANHEDRIN AND THE HIGH PRIEST CAIAPHAS
    5. THE CHIEF PRIESTS CONDEMN CHRIST
    6. JUDAS HANGS HIMSELF
    7. JESUS BEFORE PILATE
    8. JESUS BEFORE HEROD ANTIPAS
    9. CHRIST RETURNS TO PILATE

C. CHRIST HEALS THE WORLD
    1. CHRIST FLOGGED
    2. ROMAN SOLDIERS MOCK JESUS
    3. THE CRUCIFIXION
    4. RIGHTEOUS REWARD FOR THE DISPENSATION OF THE LAW

D. JESUS REMOVES THE SINS OF THE WORLD
(SIXTH DISPENSATION GRACE)
    1. JESUS JUDGES SIN
    2. JESUS DIES (ISRAEL'S TIME CLOCK STOPS UNTIL THE TRIBULATION PERIOD)
33 AD, *33 AD (U)*
    3. JESUS DESCENDS INTO THE EARTH
    4. THE BURIAL OF JESUS
    5. DAY AFTER CRUCIFIXION (SABBATH DAY)
    6. JESUS JUDGES SATAN'S KINGDOM
    7. LORDSHIP OF THE EARTH RESTORED (LAST ADAM)

E. THE RESURRECTION
33 AD, *33 AD (U)*
    1. JESUS WAS DEAD, NOW ALIVE
    2. MARY MAGDALENE AND OTHER WOMEN GO TO THE EMPTY TOMB

3. THE WOMEN ENTER THE TOMB WITHOUT MARY MAGDALENE

4. THE REST OF THE WOMEN RETURN TO TELL DISCIPLES

5. PETER AND JOHN GO TO TOMB WITH MARY MAGDALENE

6. JESUS APPEARS TO MARY MAGDALENE OUTSIDE THE TOMB

7. JESUS TAKES PARADISE TO HEAVEN

8. JESUS ENTERS THE HEAVENLY TEMPLE BY HIS BLOOD

9. JESUS RETURNS TO EARTH

10. THE GUARDS' REPORT

11. JESUS APPEARS TO PETER

12. ON THE ROAD TO EMMAUS

33 AD

13. JESUS APPEARS TO THE DISCIPLES

14. JESUS APPEARS TO THOMAS

33 AD, *33 AD (U)*

15. THE SEA OF GALILEE

16. THE GREAT COMMISSION

17. LAST JOURNEY TO JERUSALEM

18. JESUS COMMANDS DISCIPLES TO WAIT AT JERUSALEM

19. THE ASCENSION - JESUS TAKEN UP INTO HEAVEN

33 AD, *33 AD (U)*

20. DISCIPLES WORSHIP AT THE TEMPLE

21. MANY MORE THINGS NOT WRITTEN

F. THE CHURCH BEGINS AT JERUSALEM

1. MATTHIAS CHOSEN TO REPLACE JUDAS

2. THE GOSPEL STARTS IN JERUSALEM

33 AD, *33 AD (U)*

3. POWER OF EARLY CHURCH

33 AD (U)

4. CHRISTIANS PERSECUTED

5. SAUL'S CONVERSION (PAUL)

35 AD (U)

6. TIBERIUS DIES, GAIUS CALIGULA NOW EMPEROR OF ROME

37-41 AD (U)

7. JOSEPHUS BORN (WRITER OF HISTORY)

37 AD (U)

8. PAUL JOURNEYS TO JERUSALEM

37 AD (U)

9. THE CHURCH PROSPERS

      10. GAIUS CALIGULA DIES, CLAUDIUS NOW EMPEROR OF ROME

41-54 AD (U)

      11. THE GOSPEL SPREADS TO THE UTTERMOST PARTS OF THE EARTH

42 AD (U)

      12. BOOK OF JAMES

      (AUTHORED BY HALF-BROTHER OF JESUS)

      13. JAMES DIES (SON OF ZEBEDEE)

44 AD (U)

      14. HEROD AGRIPPA I DIES

44 AD (U)

      15. PAUL AND BARNABAS FULFILL THEIR MISSION IN JUDEA AND RETURN TO ANTIOCH

G. PAUL'S FIRST MISSIONARY JOURNEY
(BARNABAS ACCOMPANIES)

44-45 AD (U)

      1. JOURNEY FROM JERUSALEM TO PERGA

44 AD (U)

      2. IN PISIDIAN ANTIOCH

44 AD (U)

      3. IN ICONIUM (LYCAONIA)

      4. IN LYSTRA (LYCAONIA)

45 AD (U)

      5. THE RETURN TO ANTIOCH IN SYRIA

45 AD (U)

      6. ANTIOCH (SYRIA)

45 AD (U)

      7. THE COUNCIL AT JERUSALEM

52 AD (U)

      8. PAUL AND BARNABAS RETURN TO ANTIOCH

      9. GOSPEL OF MARK WRITTEN

H. PAUL'S SECOND MISSIONARY JOURNEY
(SILAS ACCOMPANIES)

53-56 AD (U)

      1. THE JOURNEY BEGINS FROM ANTIOCH (SYRIA)

53 AD (U)

      2. FROM DERBE TO ATHENS

53 AD (U)

      3. IN CORINTH (1 ½ YEARS)

4. PAUL LEAVES CORINTH

5. BOOK OF 1 THESSALONIANS

(AUTHORED BY PAUL AT CORINTH)

54 AD (U)

6. TIMOTHY SENT TO THESSALONICA

7. BOOK OF 2 THESSALONIANS

(AUTHORED BY PAUL AT CORINTH)

54 AD (U)

8. GAIUS CLAUDIUS DIES, NERO CLAUDIUS CAESAR AUGUSTUS NOW EMPEROR

54-68 AD (U)

9. THE END OF PAUL'S SECOND MISSIONARY JOURNEY

56 AD (U)

I. PAUL'S THIRD MISSIONARY JOURNEY

56-60 AD (U)

1. BEGINS AT ANTIOCH (SYRIA)

56 AD (U)

2. AT EPHESUS

56-58 AD (U)

3. GALATIANS QUICKLY TURN AWAY

4. PAUL'S PLANS TO VISIT ROME AND SPAIN

59 AD (U)

5. BOOK OF 1 CORINTHIANS

(AUTHORED BY PAUL AT EPHESUS)

59 AD (U)

6. TIMOTHY AND ERASTUS SENT TO MACEDONIA

7. PAUL GOES TO MACEDONIA

59 AD (U)

8. BOOK OF 2 CORINTHIANS

(AUTHORED BY PAUL IN MACEDONIA)

60 AD (U)

9. PAUL'S JOURNEY TO CORINTH

60 AD (U)

10. BOOK OF GALATIANS

(AUTHORED BY PAUL AT CORINTH)

11. BOOK OF ROMANS

(AUTHORED BY PAUL AT CORINTH)

60 AD (U)

12. PAUL'S RETURN CONCLUDES HIS THIRD MISSIONARY JOURNEY

J. PAUL ARRESTED AND FOURTH MISSIONARY JOURNEY

1. AT JERUSALEM
60 AD (U)

2. PAUL TRANSFERRED TO CAESAREA
60 AD (U)

3. GOSPELS OF MATTHEW AND LUKE WRITTEN

4. PAUL SAILS FOR ROME
62 AD (U)

5. ARRIVAL AT ROME
63 AD (U)

6. PAUL'S FIRST IMPRISONMENT IN ROME
63-65 AD (U)

7. JAMES DIES (HALF-BROTHER OF JESUS)
63 AD (U)

8. NERO WATCHES ROME BURN - CHRISTIAN PERSECUTION INCREASES
64 AD (U)

9. THE CONVERSION OF ONESIMUS

10. TIMOTHY RELEASED

11. BOOK OF PHILIPPIANS
(AUTHORED BY PAUL AT ROME)
64 AD (U)

12. BOOK OF PHILEMON
(AUTHORED BY PAUL AT ROME)
64 AD (U)

13. BOOK OF COLOSSIANS
(AUTHORED BY PAUL AT ROME)
64 AD (U)

14. BOOK OF EPHESIANS
(AUTHORED BY PAUL AT ROME)
64 AD (U)

15. TYCHICUS AND ONESIMUS DELIVER THE LETTERS

16. BOOK OF HEBREWS
(POSSIBLY AUTHORED BY PAUL AT ROME)
64 AD (U)

17. PAUL RELEASED FROM HOUSE PRISON
65 AD (U)

K. PAUL'S FINAL JOURNEY

 1. PAUL AND TIMOTHY TRAVEL TO CRETE, THEN EPHESUS

 2. LUKE WRITES THE BOOK OF ACTS

 3. BOOK OF 1 TIMOTHY

 (AUTHORED BY PAUL AT MACEDONIA)

65 AD (U)

 4. BOOK OF TITUS

 (AUTHORED BY PAUL AT MACEDONIA)

65 AD (U)

 5. PAUL'S LETTER DELIVERED TO TITUS

 6. PAUL TRAVELS BACK TO ROME

66 AD (U)

 7. PAUL BEFORE NERO

66 AD (U)

 8. BOOK OF 1 PETER

 (AUTHORED BY PETER AT ROME)

 9. PAUL AND PETER FOREWARNED OF THEIR COMING DEATHS

 10. BOOK OF 2 PETER

 (AUTHORED BY PETER AT ROME)

66 AD (U)

 11. BOOK OF 2 TIMOTHY

 (AUTHORED BY PAUL, SECOND IMPRISONMENT AT ROME)

66 AD (U)

 12. BOOK OF JUDE

 (AUTHORED BY JUDE, HALF-BROTHER OF JESUS)

 13. PERSECUTIONS OF THE EARLY CHURCH INCREASE

 14. MARTYRDOM OF PETER AND PAUL

67 AD (U)

 15. NERO CLAUDIUS CAESAR AUGUSTUS DIES

68 AD (U)

 16. VESPASIAN NOW EMPEROR OF ROME

69-79 AD

L. THE DESTRUCTION OF THE TEMPLE

 1. GENERAL TITUS PLUNDERS JERUSALEM

70 AD (U)

 2. THE HEBREWS RETURN TO SLAVERY BY ROMANS

 3. TITUS NOW EMPEROR OF ROME

79-81 AD

4. DOMITIAN NOW EMPEROR OF ROME

81-96 AD

M. JOHN'S WRITINGS

1. GOSPEL OF JOHN WRITTEN

90 AD

2. BOOK OF 1 JOHN

(AUTHORED BY JOHN)

90 AD

3. BOOK OF 2 JOHN

(AUTHORED BY JOHN)

90 AD

4. BOOK OF 3 JOHN

(AUTHORED BY JOHN)

90 AD

5. CANON OF HEBREW BIBLE CLOSED (OLD TESTAMENT)

90 AD

6. BOOK OF REVELATION

(AUTHORED BY JOHN ON PATMOS)

95 AD

7. JOHN THE LAST APOSTLE DIES

N. THE EARLY POST APOSTOLIC CHURCH

1. BAR KOKHBA REVOLT

132 AD

2. HEBREW BIBLE CANON COMPLETE

c. 200 AD

3. CONSTANTINE - FIRST CHRISTIAN EMPEROR OF ROME

306-337 AD

3. COUNCIL OF CARTHAGE

397 AD

4. JEROME TRANSLATIONS THE BIBLE INTO LATIN (THE VULGATE)

405 AD

5. ROME SACKED BY VISIGOTHS

410 AD

O. THE SPREAD OF ISLAM

1. MUHAMMAD BORN

570 AD

2. MUHAMMAD RECEIVES HIS VISION

610 AD

3. ISLAMIC WAR CONQUERS PETRA

629-632 AD

4. MUHAMMAD DIES

632 AD

P. MIDDLE AGES OF THE CHURCH

1. CHARLEMAGNE'S SCHOOL OF SEVENFOLD INSTRUCTION

800 AD

2. MASORETES

900 AD

3. ARCHBISHOP STEPHAN LANGSTON

1207 AD

4. JOHN WYCLIFFE TRANSLATES LATIN BIBLE INTO ENGLISH

1384 AD

5. JOHANNES GUTENBERG INVENTS THE PRINTING PRESS

1453 AD

6. COLUMBUS CROSSES THE ATLANTIC OCEAN

1492 AD

Q. PROTESTANT REFORMATION

1. MARTIN LUTHER

1517 AD

2. WILLIAM TYNDALE NEW TESTAMENT

(THE FIRST ENGLISH PRINTED BIBLE)

1526 AD

3. ROBERT ESTIENNE

4. GREGORIAN CALENDAR FIRST IMPLEMENTED IN SPAIN

1582 AD

5. KING JAMES

1551 AD

6. ARCHBISHOP USSHER'S '*THE ANNALS OF THE WORLD*' PUBLISHED

1658 AD (U)

7. MARK TWAIN STATES, "ISRAEL IS A DESOLATE WASTELAND"

1867 AD

8. HEBREW LANGUAGE REBORN

R. WORLD WAR I

(THE POLITICAL WAR)

1914-1918 AD

    1. GENERAL ALLENBY UTILIZES AIRPLANES TO DELIVER JERUSALEM

1917 AD

S. WORLD WAR II
(THE ETHNIC WAR)

1939-1945 AD

    1. ISRAEL'S RESTORATION INCREASES

1948 AD

    2. PARABLE OF THE FIG TREE (ISRAEL)

1948 AD

    3. THE PEOPLE OF ISRAEL RETURN TO THEIR LAND

    4. PROSPERITY OF MOAB AND AMMON (JORDAN) RESTORED

1960's AD

    5. THE PLOT AGAINST ISRAEL

1967 AD

    6. THE NEW INTERNATIONAL VERSION (NIV) BIBLE PUBLISHED

1978 AD

    7. GOG (RULER OF DARKNESS) TURNED BACK

1982 AD

    8. ISRAEL OCCUPIES FROM NEGEV TO ZAREPHATH

1982-2004 AD

    9. NO KING IN ISRAEL UNTIL MESSIAH RETURNS

    10. THE PRODUCTIVITY OF ISRAEL'S LAND RESTORED

    11. THE FORMER AND LATTER RAINS

    12. MILITARY BABYLON (IRAQ) DESTROYED

2003 AD

    13. INTERNAL PALESTINIAN CONFLICT

T. CURRENT DAY

    1. THE PLAN BIBLE PUBLISHES *'THE PLAN'*

2010 AD

    2. UNDERSTANDING INCREASES IN THE LATTER DAYS

    3. THE COMMAND OF THE LORD'S SUPPER UNTIL HE RETURNS

    4. WHAT THE CHURCH MUST DO

    5. LIKE THE DAYS OF NOAH

    6. MOCKERS CRY OUT AGAINST THE SECOND COMING

    7. HUMANITY'S SINFUL RESPONSE DURING GRACE DISPENSATION

    8. ANTICHRIST RESTRAINED BY THE HOLY SPIRIT IN THE CHURCH

9. THE SIGNS OF THE END OF THE CHURCH AGE

10. THE GREATEST REVIVAL OF ALL TIME

U. WORLD WAR III
(THE RELIGIOUS WAR)

1. ORACLES AGAINST DAMASCUS

2. DESTRUCTION OF ISRAEL'S CLOSEST ENEMIES

3. THE WAR (BATTLE OF GOG AND MAGOG)

4. WINNING THE BATTLE OF GOG AND MAGOG

5. EXODUS II INCREASES

6. THE GOSPEL PREACHED TO ALL NATIONS

V. END OF THE CHURCH AGE - CHRIST COMES FOR THE FAITHFUL BRIDE

1. THE FAITHFUL BRIDE PREPARES FOR HIS SECOND COMING

2. CHRIST ALWAYS WITH US

3. OUR BODIES GROAN, AWAITING THE COMPLETION OF SALVATION

4. FIRST RESURRECTION (SALVATION OF THE BODY) BEGINS

5. FAITHFUL LIVING BELIEVERS ARE CAUGHT UP INTO HEAVEN (FIRST RAPTURE)

6. FAITHFUL OVERCOMERS DO NOT ENDURE THE TRIBULATION PERIOD

7. BELIEVERS' WORKS REWARDED IN HEAVEN

8. THE BELIEVERS' REWARDS AND CROWNS IN HEAVEN

9. JESUS PRESENTS HIS FAITHFUL BRIDE TO THE FATHER

10. JESUS IS WORTHY TO OPEN THE SEALED BOOK IN HEAVEN

XI. CONSTERNATION - TRIBULATION PERIOD: *Seven Years*

A. THE FIRST HALF OF THE SEVEN YEARS

1. DANIEL'S SEVENTIETH WEEK (ISRAEL'S TIME CLOCK STARTS AGAIN)

Seven Years Left of Satan's Kingdom

2. THE MAN WHO IS THE ANTICHRIST REVEALED - THE WHITE HORSE (FIRST SEAL)

3. THE KINGDOM OF THE ANTICHRIST CHARACTERISTICS

4. ISRAEL STARTS TO SEE THE MESSIAH

5. THE ANGELS HOLD BACK THE WINDS UNTIL SERVANTS ARE SEALED

6. THE 144,000 ISRAELITE EVANGELISTS PREACH THE GOSPEL

7. ANTICHRIST (THE BEAST) RISES QUICKLY TO POWER - A SYSTEM AND A MAN

8. ANTICHRIST MAKES SEVEN YEAR COVENANT WITH ISRAEL AND OTHERS

9. THE NATIONS ARE IN TURMOIL

10. THE FALSE PROPHET - A SYSTEM AND A MAN

B. THE MIDDLE OF THE TRIBULATION PERIOD

1. CHOSEN LIVING BELIEVERS ARE CAUGHT UP INTO HEAVEN (SECOND RAPTURE)

Mid-Tribulation

2. THE GOSPEL OF SALVATION PREACHED BY AN ANGEL

3. WAR IN HEAVENS (LASTS ONE DAY)
4. WAR ON EARTH - ANTICHRIST TURNS FROM PEACE - RED HORSE (SECOND SEAL)

5. ANTICHRIST ABOLISHES THE SACRIFICE

1,290 Days Left of Satan's Kingdom

6. MARRIAGE SUPPER OF THE LAMB IN HEAVEN

C. THE GREAT TRIBULATION PERIOD - SECOND THREE AND HALF YEARS

1. NO TIME AS THIS BEFORE OR AFTER

2. SATAN AND THE ANTICHRIST TRY TO CHANGE GOD'S SET TIME

3. ANTICHRIST OPPRESSES ISRAELITES AND NEW CONVERTS

Three and Half Years Left of Satan's Kingdom

4. ANTICHRIST'S HEADQUARTERS AT JERUSALEM

5. FALSE PROPHET SETS UP ANTICHRIST IMAGE IN THE TEMPLE

6. ISRAEL FLEES TO THE WILDERNESS

7. ISRAEL STAYS IN THE WILDERNESS FOR 3½ YEARS

1,260 Days Israel in the Wilderness

8. SATAN FRUSTRATED - FLOOD ATTEMPT ON ISRAEL

9. THE TWO WITNESSES PREACH THE GOSPEL FOR 3 ½ YEARS

10. THE ANTICHRIST WOUNDED IN BATTLE

11. FALSE RELIGION TRANSFORMED INTO ANTICHRIST WORSHIP

12. WORLDWIDE FAMINE - BLACK HORSE (THIRD SEAL)

13. FALSE PROPHET'S ECONOMIC SOLUTION

14. ANTICHRIST AND FALSE PROPHET DECEIVE THROUGH COUNTERFEIT SIGNS

15. DEATH OVER ONE FOURTH OF THE EARTH - PALE HORSE (FOURTH SEAL)

16. ANTICHRIST OVERPOWERS SECOND HALF TRIBULATION CONVERTS

17. JACOB'S DISTRESS

18. TWO THIRDS OF ISRAEL CUT OFF

19. BLESSED ARE THE MARTYRS IN CHRIST FROM NOW ON (FIFTH SEAL)

20. PRAYERS OF BELIEVERS ANSWERED WITH THUNDER, LIGHTNING, EARTHQUAKE

21. TWO WITNESSES CALL DOWN TRUMPETS AND PLAGUES

22. SOUNDING OF THE FIRST FOUR TRUMPETS (NATURAL DISASTERS)

23. FIFTH TRUMPET - ANGEL OPENS THE ABYSS

One Year and Six Months Left of Satan's Kingdom

24. SIXTH TRUMPET - NUCLEAR WAR

One Year Left of Satan's Kingdom

25. HUMANITY UNREPENTANT

26. ISRAEL CONTINUES TO BE PROTECTED

27. RESURRECTED BELIEVERS (SEA OF GLASS) AND SOULS OF TRIBULATION MARTYRS (IN HEAVEN)

28. PLAGUES ON THE NATIONS (BOWLS POURED OUT)

One Month Left of Satan's Kingdom

29. LIKE THE DAYS OF NOAH

30. TRIBULATION CONVERTS HATED BECAUSE OF JESUS

D. GLORIOUS APPEARANCE OF JESUS CHRIST

Ten Days Left of Satan's Kingdom

1. NO MORE DELAY

2. SEVENTH TRUMPET PREPARED - THE MYSTERY OF GOD IS FINISHED

3. JESUS SEEN BY ALL IN THE CLOUDS

4. GATHERING OF THE END OF TRIBULATION CONVERTS

5. AFTER SEEING JESUS' GLORIOUS APPEARANCE, ISRAEL REPENTS

6. THE ISRAELITES RETURN TO JERUSALEM

7. JERUSALEM ATTACKED

8. THE SEVEN THUNDERS (NOT WRITTEN DOWN)

9. TWO WITNESSES RESURRECTED (SECOND WOE)

9. THE SEVEN THUNDERS (NOT WRITTEN DOWN)

E. THE DAY OF GOD'S WRATH

Last Day of Satan's Kingdom

1. LAST DAY OF THE TRIBULATION PERIOD
2. SIXTH SEAL - GREAT EARTHQUAKE (MANTLE PLUME ERUPTION)
3. SIGNS IN THE SKY
4. GREATEST EARTHQUAKE EVER (CONTINENTS SHIFT)
5. ALL WHO CALL UPON THE LORD ARE SAVED, THAT DID NOT TAKE THE MARK
6. SILENCE IN HEAVEN FOR THIRTY MINUTES (SEVENTH SEAL)

F. THE GREAT DAY OF THE LORD - JESUS RETURNS TO EARTH

Satan's Kingdom Ends

1. THE ANCIENT OF DAYS (GOD THE FATHER)
2. THE LORD'S PREPARATION TO RETURN
3. THE LORD MOUNTS A WHITE HORSE, ARMIES ARE WITH HIM
4. THE RETURN IS LIKE LIGHTNING
5. THE LORD RETURNS IN GREAT POWER AND GLORY
6. THE LORD RETURNS TO EARTH ON THE MOUNT OF OLIVES
7. THE BEGINNING OF THE GREAT WINEPRESS OF THE LORD
8. THE LORD ENTERS JERUSALEM
9. THE LORD'S ARMY RIDES NORTH TOWARD MEGIDDO (ARMAGEDDON)
10. THE BATTLE OF ARMAGEDDON
11. JESUS IS THE STONE THAT DESTROYS THE ANTICHRIST'S KINGDOM
12. ANGELS HARVEST THE WICKED - THE END OF THE GREAT WINEPRESS

62

A. JUDGMENT OF THE LIVING (ON EARTH)

First 44 Days of the Millennial Reign

1. DANIEL'S SEVENTIETH WEEK FINISHED (ISRAEL'S TIME CLOCK COMPLETED)
2. THE ISRAELITES WHO MAKE IT THROUGH THE TRIBULATION
3. CHRIST'S THRONE ON EARTH
4. SATAN'S KINGDOM REMOVED FROM THE EARTH
5. ANGELS GATHER ALL LIVING TO BE JUDGED
6. THE LAST OF THE FIRST RESURRECTION (ON EARTH)
7. EVERY KNEE OF THE LIVING SHALL BOW
8. THOSE WHO TOOK THE ANTICHRIST'S MARK JUDGED
9. THE NATIONS SEPARATED INTO SHEEP AND GOATS
10. JESUS' ENEMIES MADE HIS FOOTSTOOL
11. THE LORD AND HIS BELIEVERS TAKE POSSESSION OF THE KINGDOM

WORLD SUPREMACY BELONGS TO JESUS CHRIST

12. FEAST OF THE KINGDOM ON THE EARTH
13. REWARDS OF THE KINGDOM ON EARTH
14. THE CURSE OF THE LAND REMOVED
15. RIGHTEOUS REWARD FROM THE DISPENSATION OF GRACE

B. THE MILLENNIAL REIGN - THE KINGDOM OF OUR LORD

One Thousand Years

(SEVENTH DISPENSATION - MESSIANIC)

1. JESUS REIGNS FROM JERUSALEM, THE CAPITAL OF THE EARTH
2. THE TWELVE DISCIPLES JUDGE THE TWELVE TRIBES
3. DAVID IS KING OF ISRAEL
4. NATURAL ISRAEL IN THE KINGDOM (TRIBULATION SURVIVORS)
5. ISRAEL'S INITIAL LAND GRANT OF THE MILLENNIAL REIGN
6. THE NATIONS IN THE KINGDOM (NON-ISRAELITE TRIBULATION SURVIVORS)
7. SIN DURING THE MILLENNIAL REIGN
8. WAR IS ENDED
9. PALESTINIAN RECONCILIATION
10. MILLENNIAL TEMPLE BUILT NORTH OF JERUSALEM
11. THE TEMPLE DEDICATION - THE GLORY RETURNS TO THE TEMPLE
12. MILLENNIAL TEMPLE ORDER OF WORSHIP
13. MILLENNIAL RIVER FROM THE TEMPLE THROUGH JERUSALEM
14. FRUIT TREES YIELD FRUIT TWELVE MONTHS OF THE YEAR

XIII. CONDEMNATION - THE GREAT WHITE THRONE: *One Thousand Years Ends*

A. SATAN'S DOOM

1. SATAN BOUND FOR 1,000 YEARS (MILLENNIAL REIGN)
2. JUDGMENT FOR SINFUL RESPONSE DURING THE MESSIANIC DISPENSATION
3. SATAN'S FINAL DESTRUCTION
4. HEAVEN AND EARTH WEAR OUT LIKE AN OLD GARMENT

B. JUDGMENT OF THE WICKED DEAD - THE GREAT WHITE THRONE

1. JESUS SITS ON THE GREAT WHITE THRONE
2. THE SECOND RESURRECTION (THE DEAD)
3. THE BOOKS ARE OPENED
4. EVERY KNEE OF THE WICKED DEAD SHALL BOW
5. NO REDEMPTION PLAN FOR FALLEN ANGELS WHO CHOSE WITHOUT TEMPTATION
6. THE SECOND DEATH

C. HEAVEN AND EARTH RENOVATED BY FIRE

1. SECOND DEATH HAS NO POWER OVER BELIEVERS FROM FIRST RESURRECTION
2. DEATH IS THE LAST ENEMY DESTROYED
3. CHRIST DELIVERS UP HIS KINGDOM TO THE FATHER
4. HEAVEN AND EARTH RENOVATED BY FIRE

A. GOD'S 7,000 YEAR PLAN COMPLETED – GOD AND HUMANITY DWELL TOGETHER

1. NEW HEAVEN AND NEW EARTH

2. THE NEW JERUSALEM - THE CAPITAL OF THE UNIVERSE

3. CHANNELS OF ETERNAL LIFE (TREE AND RIVER OF LIFE)

4. GOD AND HUMANITY DWELL TOGETHER FOREVER

5. ATTRIBUTES OF THE ETERNAL KINGDOM

6. ALL OF THE CURSE, CAUSED BY SIN OF HUMANITY, COMPLETELY REMOVED FOREVER

7. THE BLESSING TO 1,000 GENERATIONS

(1,000 GENERATIONS REQUIRE MORE THAN 7,000 YEARS)

B. ETERNAL AGES TO COME

1. JESUS RULES AND REIGNS FOREVER

2. JESUS IS OUR HIGH PRIEST FOREVER

3. THE BRIDE REIGNS FOREVER AS ONE

(RESURRECTED CHURCH AND ISRAEL)

4. ISRAEL LOVED FOREVER

5. NATURAL PEOPLE REPRODUCE FOREVER

6. HUMANITY FILLS THE UNIVERSE WITH THE LORD

7. STARS NEVER PASS AWAY

8. THE BLESSING CONTINUES THROUGH ALL GENERATIONS

9. GOD'S ETERNAL RELATIONSHIP WITH HUMANITY

10. GOD GLORIFIED FOREVER

Soli Deo Gloria in Aeternum.